THE VOYAGE
OF THE ULUA

THE VOYAGE OF THE ULUA

by ARIE L. ELIAV

Translated from the Hebrew
by ISRAEL I. TASLITT

A SABRA BOOK
FUNK AND WAGNALLS
NEW YORK

LIBRARY OF CONGRESS CATALOG CARD NUMBER 69-13468
PRINTED IN ISRAEL

For Tanya

"Ulua" was the Latin American name of the Haganah immigrant ship, *"Haim Arlosoroff."*

I gave this book its foreign name because during most of its wanderings and adventures the vessel bore the name "Ulua".

This story does not purport to be an official document. It is not based on any research in archives. The names of some of the people and places have certainly dimmed with the passage of time—some two decades.

If one of the immigrants, or seamen, or escorts had sat down to write about the events that I have recalled, the story would surely have been told from quite another perspective.

I hope that the book casts some light on the people of my generation, in their finest hour.

A.L.E.

Contents

CONTENTS

*We were lying at the mouth of the Gulf of Taranto. The year—*1947.

We purposely slowed the pace of the "Ulua," intending to reach Gallipoli harbor at dark. We had no desire to attract undue attention.

All preparations for the night operation were done. The hundreds of refugees from Sweden lay sprawled on the wooden bunks in the ship's hold, resting after a day of hard labor. The American and Spanish sailors were preoccupied with their own affairs. The Palyam *men were in the wireless room, making conversation.*

I stood on the bridge and looked into the far distance, to the tip of the Italian toe, thinking. A strange destiny bound me to the Gulf of Taranto.

Several years earlier, in 1943, *I came to the Gulf on a large, ocean-going liner, converted by the British Navy into a troop carrier. Aboard were thousands of soldiers, men from British, Palestinian, Indian and African units. I was one of them. We had been transported from Port Said to the Allied bridgehead at the southern tip of the Italian boot. We sailed in a large convoy; our escorts were destroyers, frigates, corvettes and mine-sweepers. Our ship, originally a passenger liner, was also armed with anti-aircraft cannon and machine guns. As we entered the Gulf, I gazed alternately at the skies and in the direction of the harbor.*

Early in 1946, *I once again sailed into the Gulf. This time I stood on the bridge of the tiny wooden Turkish vessel* Bodrum. *Menahem ("Churchill") was at the helm. Mario was the navigator. Fabi, Bezalel, Uri and Haim, the* Palmach *fellows were below with Damini, Ricardo, Gino and the other sailors who were helping us. They were keeping an eye on the vessel's whimpering Turkish owners. Lucia was waiting ashore.*

And now, on the bridge of the "Ulua," I wondered: "What is Lucia doing tonight, that Italian Rahab of ours?"

My thoughts went back to the refugees of the "Ulua," their fate and future, then to my beloved Tanya, huddled there in the hold of the ship with her hundreds of companions. "If ever we reach our land," I promised myself, "I will take her to the Kinneret. We'll live there until we build a home of our own. We'll rest, if only for a brief spell."

I am going to tell, again, how I got to be at the mouth of the Gulf of Taranto. Where had my long voyage begun? Was it in the boy scout shack by the blue sea and golden sands of Tel Aviv? Or on guard duty in starlit Sh'feya and Ben-Shemen? Perhaps it began with the heavy shore batteries at the edge of Bat-Galim or the mighty military installations we built at Port Taufik and Port Fuad. Or perhaps, in the dusty convoy routes of the western desert, between Tobruk and Bengazi. But all these are stories by themselves. I shall begin, therefore, with the day I came back to my homeland, after the War.

PART ONE

PRELUDE TO THE ULUA

Kalkilya

In 1945, mustered out of the British Army, I went to Kibbutz Kinneret to join my army buddies whose home the settlement was. It was the harvest season, and every morning at dawn I went out to cut the wheat. After all the years of knocking about in the army, working on the combine in the blazing sun along the shores of the Sea of Galilee was, for me, a form of therapy. I would return from the fields dead tired, take a shower and fall asleep. Sweet is the slumber of the toiler, and I savored that sweetness to the full.

From the Jordan Valley we went on to harvest the fields of Kinneret and Ein Gev in the Madar and Olam lands on the hills of Lower Galilee. Ours was a small group, equipped with tractors and combines. We lived the open life in shacks, working by day and standing guard at night.

When the harvest season was over, I returned to Tel Aviv and reported to Haganah headquarters. I was placed in charge of Haganah intelligence in the Northern Sharon District. My main job was to keep track of British Army and Police movements. The bitter struggle had already begun over the issue of immigration. The British had concentrated substantial forces on the Mount Carmel slopes and in the Northern Sharon-Atlit area, near Zichron Yaacov, Pardes Hanna, Hadera. We tried to infiltrate their camps with agents to keep us informed about troop dispositions and movements. We also kept track of the British Police in Northern Sharon and the coastal stations.

I well recall how we came into possession of the secret code used by the Police. Kapi was a veteran cab driver in Hadera. His Ford was always in good shape and ready for action. Kapi was widely known in the town, something of an institution. There wasn't a house or resident that he didn't know. He was aware of everything that happened within range of his cab, including the surrounding

Arab villages. He knew hundreds of Arab villagers by name. He was at home in the British Army camps in Northern Sharon and in the British police stations. He was also a Haganah man and a member of its intelligence service. He never hesitated to accept an assignment. He was always in good spirits. He did his job with that special ease which comes with many years of driving a cab in a small town, a calling which enables a man to be at one and the same time a hail-fellow-well-met, a confessional priest and an amateur detective.

About six o'clock one evening, having shaved, showered and dressed, I was ready for our assignment. Again I counted the money I had received at Haganah intelligence headquarters, and placed the white envelope in the breast pocket of my jacket. Kapi called for me in his car and we started out. We neared the Kalkilya police station at dark, and Kapi parked the car off the road several hundred yards away, in the shelter of a eucalyptus grove, but left his parking lights burning. We sat in the cab for about ten minutes. Nothing happened. The road was dark and deserted. We could see the lights twinkling in the police station and on the fence posts surrounding it. From a nearby grove came the monotonous grunt of a well-pump, only emphasizing the surrounding silence. I glanced at my watch.

"He should be here any minute," I said. "I was told he'd be punctual. I'm getting into the back seat. When he comes, open the rear door for him. It's best that he sit with me."

A moment later we heard footsteps. A tall man approached us and Kapi opened the door. The man got in and sat down beside me.

"Where are we going?" he asked me in English.

"To Fiddler's, in Kfar Saba. He's waiting for us in the back room."

"Good. Let's go."

Out of the corner of one eye, as Kapi drove, I studied the profile of the man beside me. Something was wrong. I had been told that the sergeant would be in mufti, but here he was in police uniform, his police cap on his lap.

In a few minutes we were in the center of Kfar Saba. Kapi drove into the back yard of the Fiddler's Cafe Restaurant. The sergeant remained in the car.

"Wait a minute," I said. "I'll see if the room is ready."

Fiddler opened the door. "You can come in," he said. "No one will disturb you. I'm at your service."

Kapi stayed with the car.

The sergeant and I faced each other across a table. "Good," he said. "First let's have a drink."

Fiddler came in and the sergeant ordered brandy. At headquarters I had been told he would hand the material over only after he had drunk a good deal. "Let him drink, and drink along with him until he's drunk." We drank brandy and talked about women. Then we drank some more brandy and talked about more women. He ordered beer, more brandy, more beer. An hour went by. My stomach was heaving and my head was growing heavy. Every fifteen minutes or so, the sergeant stepped out to the toilet to relieve himself. I went outside, thrust two fingers down my throat and vomited my entrails out, then rinsed my face under the faucet in the yard and went back in.

We continued to drink. I could hardly see the sergeant through the veil of alcohol. Again I went out to wash my face in the cool water. I was dripping with sweat. Every time I went out I could see Kapi standing by his Ford, following my movements with his eyes.

Two more hours passed, and I knew I wouldn't be able to keep it up much longer. All the while, the sergeant kept his cold blue eyes fixed on me. Gradually they became clouded, watery.

"Did you bring the money?" he suddenly demanded.

"Yes. I have it here."

"Fine. Let's have another drink."

Then, as from some far-off infinity, I heard him say: "Here's the bloody thing. Take it!"

He thrust a small square bit of paper at me across the table. I had a hard time holding it steady. The letters danced before my eyes. I identified the sheet by the three marks I had been told about at headquarters. I took out the envelope and slid it across to the sergeant. He glanced into it and, without bothering to count the notes, shoved it into the pocket of his jacket. With some difficulty we managed to get up from the table. The Ford's motor was already running when we climbed in. It was almost midnight, Kapi said.

He drove fast. The wind slapped at our faces through the open windows, reviving me from my stupor. Kapi brought the car to a halt about fifty yards away from the police station.

"Here we are," I said to the sergeant.

He had also managed to sober up a bit. "Help me out," he muttered, staring at me. "I'm having trouble."

I got out and helped him. He seized my arm with a grip of iron and began pulling me toward the station. I could not shake myself loose.

"Let me go," I said.

He thrust me away and drew his service revolver. "Now I'll shoot you like a dog," he cried. "You thought I'd turn traitor for money." His voice sounded cool and crisp. The revolver was pointing at my chest, and his finger was on the trigger. In those long seconds, everything seemed preternaturally clear: the sergeant's hand, the gunsight, the bullets glinting in the cylinder. The revolver rose slowly until it was at the level of my eyes.

"Come on, stop joking," I said, gently laying my hand on his arm and slowly pressing it down.

"No," the sergeant insisted. "I'm going to shoot you like a dog." But now there was a weariness in his voice. The revolver was waist-high, and I was still pressing his arm down.

"Easy does it," I said.

"No," he said thickly. "I want to kill you."

I guided the hand with the revolver toward the holster. He was now leaning on me with his full weight. "I want to kill you," he whimpered. "Let me kill you. I'm a traitor." I led him a few steps toward the station, then let him stagger on to the gate.

I made it back to the car, sank down on the rear seat and blacked out.

It was about an hour after midnight when Kapi delivered me, shaky and streaked with vomit, to the home of our commander. I took out the sheet of paper and handed it to him; it was the key to the British Police code for that month. Dimly I heard Kapi telling the commander what had happened.

"Fine," remarked the commander. "The important thing is that the material is in our hands. Get yourself some sleep, Lova."

Kapi put his arm around me, got me to my room, undressed me, helped me to bed and put a damp towel on my forehead.

"Let me alone," I remember saying to him. "Get some sleep."

"Arthur"

I HAD been engaged in espionage for about half a year when, late in 1945, I reported to Shaul, head of the blockade-running organization, and volunteered for service with him. I had known Shaul while still a boy, back in the days of the 1936 disturbances. I was a bicycle courier at Haganah headquarters, where he was then serving.

The report he received on my work in the intelligence service was satisfactory. He knew that I was acquainted with the Middle East and Italy from my service in the artillery and engineering units of the British Army. He put me to work in "Mossad Aliya Bet," the Haganah unit that organized "illegal" immigration and blockade-running operations.

Shaul sent me to Moshe, who was in charge of Mossad headquarters. Moshe—short, agile, extremely likeable, the friend of everyone in the organization—was the key figure in the nerve center of the operations network. Mossad headquarters was located in two rooms of a rooftop dwelling in an old building on Allenby Road in Tel Aviv, between Rothschild Boulevard and Yehuda Halevi Street. Mossad was growing and expanding. Branches were being formed in most European and Middle East countries to organize the exodus and the *aliya*. These branches needed many people—organizers and directors provided by Mossad, seamen from Palyam (Palmach's naval arm) to sail the ships, and wireless operators ("Gideonites," we called them) to maintain constant contact between headquarters, our offices in foreign countries and our ships at sea.

I now had to have a new name, by which I would henceforth be known in my blockade-running work. The reservoir of common names had already been depleted. Avigail and Avishag, Moshe's two charming secretaries, came to my aid. They consulted the telephone book for a name which would be equally easy to pronounce in Hebrew and in foreign languages, yet would not be too obvious. They decided on Arthur, and "Arthur" I became.

Atlit

Mossad was wrestling with two problems: how to repatriate the Italian seamen captured on our immigrant ships and how to get our own people—seamen, wireless operators and other Mossad men —to Italy and to our European branch offices. The Italian seamen had been held with the immigrants in the Atlit prison camp, their identity unknown to the police. Released with the others, they were placed in various settlements. The nine sailors of the *Enzo Sereni,* for instance, were living in Kibbutz Yagur, and six from the *Wingate* were being sheltered in the Immigrant Home in Binyamina. They had no complaint about the hospitality, but naturally longed to go home to their *signoras* and *signorinas*. Moreover, our branch in Italy kept calling urgently for their return to active duty.

Ada solved both problems. *Ada* was a fifty-ton vessel, powered by sail and motor, which plied between ports in Syria, Cyprus, Egypt and Eretz-Yisrael *on various missions whose nature I wouldn't care to vouch for. The owner and master was a Jew from one of our settlements. In return for substantial remuneration, he was prepared to use his vessel for ferry service on our Eretz-Yisrael-Italy route.

Just before the Passover holiday, as we were beginning to negotiate with the captain, we received word of the disaster at La Spezia, where the British halted and captured a convoy of trucks filled with refugees on their way to the port. Some of our people were arrested. Mossad headquarters in Eretz-Yisrael was concerned over the fate of the Italian branch, but our information was sketchy, and we could not estimate the extent of the damage. We decided that the *Ada* should sail immediately with the fifteen Italian seamen from the *Enzo* and the *Wingate,* three Palyam men and two wireless operators, under the command of a Mossad man—Arthur.

The day before Passover, a Sunday morning, Uri, Haim and I

* Eretz-Yisrael: the Land of Israel. Term used by the Jewish community before the establishment of Israel in 1948.

set out from Tel Aviv to Haifa. Uri and Haim were two young "Gideonites". Uri, a one-year veteran of the headquarters communication network, was about twenty, tall and lean, a farmer from one of the older southern villages. He had become a wireless operator while serving with the supernumerary police force. Haim was a newcomer to Mossad. He was Uri's age, a native of Tel Aviv and a Palmach trainee, a muscular young man with a small blond mustache and a genial smile. Now he was all tension and anticipation for the European adventure.

We went to Kibbutz Ma'apilim, south of Atlit, to select the point where we would board the *Ada*. Our first meeting with Yaacov, her master-owner, impressed us favorably. He described where he would moor his craft and worked out the details of taking aboard the men and equipment from the boat basin of the kibbutz.

We returned to Haifa where, at local Mossad headquarters, I met Menahem, whose nickname was "Churchill." He was the first of the three Palyam seamen who were to join me: born on the soil, broad-shouldered, medium height, muscular body, snub nose, wavy blond hair. We drove immediately to Hazor'im near Ein Harod for the second Palyam man. I can't say that he expected us. Fabi knew that some day he would be called up for some kind of duty, but until we descended upon him he knew nothing of the *Ada* operation. We gave him a few minutes to pack his things and make his farewells. Fabi was about my age (twenty-four) and had himself come to Eretz-Yisrael as an "illegal" immigrant just before the war.

The three of us drove to the Immigrant House in Binyamina to pick up the Italian sailors from the *Wingate*. Mario, their leader and captain, enjoyed our complete trust; he had proved himself when he brought his ship to the shores of Eretz-Yisrael. We put him in charge of the *Enzo* seamen as well, their captain having been captured by the British and held in Acre Prison. Much to my relief, I found that Mario could speak some English and German. My own Italian was so scant that I could well use Mario as an interpreter.

The men were quartered in Ma'apilim until sailing time on the following day. I went back to Haifa and met Bezalel, the third Palyam man, a tall young fellow who was a graduate of a Tel Aviv high school and a member of the Hulata fishing kibbutz. We drove up to the Hadar HaCarmel business center and outfitted ourselves with the clothes we would need in Europe—hats, ties and other accessories.

We also purchased elaborate watches with complicated dials and indicators for our seamen and wireless operators.

We reached the kibbutz just before nightfall, when the road curfew went into effect. There we found the entire contingent—not only all the passengers, equipment and food supplies, but also quite a few Palyam cadets and Palmach commanders who had come to help us to set sail.

Supper in the kibbutz mess-hall that night was something to remember. The kibbutz hadn't seen such excitement for a long time. Under the mellowing influence of *vino* (and the prospect of going back home), the Italians treated us to a series of sea chanteys. In fact, it took some effort to pry them away. We still had all the equipment to load on to the kibbutz fishing boats. Davidka, the director of our Haifa headquarters, arrived and introduced me formally to his charges, the happy Italian seamen.

"If all goes well," he said, bidding us a heartfelt *shalom,* "you'll be in Italy in six or seven days."

We collected the Italian sailors' documents, and all of them were "converted," if in name only, on the spot: Yehuda ben-Yaacov, Yossef Ezra, Avraham Levy, and so on—all good names from the Good Book to which they could take no exception. If captured, we would be a group of survivors from a foundering ship who had been picked up by the *Ada* on the high seas. Davidka gave me a few final instructions. We were to reach Italy within six to ten days, proceeding by the shortest route—from Haifa to Crete and thence to the port of Termoli on the western coast of the Adriatic, between Brindisi and Ancona. One of our men would be waiting for us in Termoli. I had to memorize a list of names and addresses in Italy. Because we were pressed for time and had to leave quickly, we did not get any wireless equipment. Davidka gave me a bundle of cash as an emergency fund. It turned out to be a minor king's ransom: dollars, pounds sterling, several hundred thousand lire and forty-five English sovereigns—small but heavy gold coins whose satisfying ring, we knew, had no peer when it came to transactions connected with smuggling and bribery. I crammed this fortune into a thick leather money-belt which I never removed until our mission was over.

Early morning found us all on the beach, concealing ourselves among the rocks. Yaacov was to meet us at eight. The waves rose higher, and so did the concern of the seamen. Finally the *Ada* hove into sight from the north and cast anchor about a hundred yards offshore. As soon as the vessel appeared, the cadets shoved out, but couldn't get their small craft past the high waves. The experienced fishermen of the kibbutz then took a hand and got the boat out into open water. Three times the boat went back and forth until all the men and equipment were aboard.

As the boat was ferrying its second load, a small one-seater plane appeared, circled above us, then leveled off and departed. We could not identify the plane, but its appearance at that precise moment did not exactly cause us any jubilation.

The "Ada"

WHEN I boarded the *Ada,* she was rocking like a nutshell. Yaacov was on the small bridge astern and ordered his crew, three Arab seamen, to weigh anchor. The anchor, however, had caught in the rocks. Our seamen lent a hand, but the anchor stayed where it was. From the shore we kept getting signals to get under way. We knew that a British destroyer would soon be coming by on blockade patrol. Yaacov and his crew kept up a steady stream of invective. After a few more attempts, we decided to abandon the anchor.

Our voyage thus began, so to speak, on the wrong foot. We sailed with only one anchor. The sea grew rough and the vessel pitched about like a drunkard. The men made themselves as comfortable as they could in the only cargo hold, among the fuel drums and food crates. The two young "Gideonites," at sea for the first time, became violently seasick and stayed in that unhappy condition until we reached Cyprus. Nor were the others in much better state.

I established myself in Captain Yaacov's cabin astern. The cabin had two dirty bunks, one of which was permanently occupied by a cat of nondescript color. A wrinkled and discolored map of the Mediterranean region, published by the German Admiralty, covered one wall of the cabin. This map served Yaacov as the springboard for many a tall tale of impressive bravery and hair-raising adventure. The cabin also boasted a wardrobe in which hung a uniform, resplendent with gold braid and dubious medals, of which Yaacov was peacock-proud.

Yaacov was born in one of the Sharon villages. He went to sea as a boy, and his adventures easily equalled those of Jack London and Joseph Conrad, combined. As far as his exploits in the Second World War were concerned, no medals could do them justice. And now, he was giving up everything "for Zionism and Aliya Bet." And at what risk! "But for you, dear friends, I will do anything."

Yes, Yaacov was brimming with pathos.

At the wheel was Abdullah, the crew's oldest member. His age was anybody's guess. He had been knocking about the eastern Mediterranean for a good half-century. He could neither read nor write, he couldn't read a map to save his life, but he was familiar with every reef and cove along these shores and he could speak all the dialects of that part of the world. Yacoub, a young Lebanese, served as the engineer and considered himself the complete intellectual. He was sure that none understood the workings of the motor better than he did. The third member of the crew was Abed, the spry, curly-haired thirteen-year-old cabin boy.

I asked Yacoub about his course. He explained that he was heading the *Ada* toward Paphos harbor at the southwestern tip of Cyprus, which her manifest indicated as her destination. We would veer off toward Crete only when beyond the cruising range of the British destroyers in the area. I took the opportunity to clarify the division of authority aboard. He was responsible to me for the progress of the ship. I would consult with Mario and our three Palyam men. Final decisions were to be made by me.

All that day our men sprawled where they had bedded down in the ship's hold. They could not stand the sight of food. During the night, the sea, far from subsiding, grew even stormier. In the morning, Yaacov suggested that we put in at one of the deserted coves along the Cypriote coast east of Limassol until the storm blew over. I took counsel with Mario, who agreed, and added that the *Ada* was too light and none too stable. Apparently no one had thought of taking on ballast.

Toward evening of the second day, we sailed into an isolated cove and dropped anchor. Yaacov and Abdullah were familiar with this cove from previous voyages. It was pleasant to ride at anchor in the serene cove following our tussle with the rough seas. Our spirits recovered and so did our appetites. The men revived.

Mario served as the link between the Italians and our men. He was about thirty, of medium height, with brown hair and a snub nose. His ruddy cheeks and round face made him look younger than he was. He talked a lot, but he wasn't a bore. And he knew his business. During the war, as an officer on an Italian submarine, he had come into contact with German officers and learned their language. Everyone immediately became fond of him and his stories.

He told me how he had come to work for "Aliya Bet." One day

he read in an Italian newspaper about the arrest of some Italian seamen near the shores of Palestine for smuggling Jews into that country. He was then without a job. The idea appealed to him, both as adventure and as a means of livelihood; someone had to be paying for the operation. But how was he to make contact? Mario reasoned that the operation was being run by Jews from the Holy Land, in which case what better contact could he make than with those serving in the British units in Italy? He probed further and learned that these soldiers had a club of their own in Milan (which also served as a center for our people in their blockade-running activities). Mario asked the soldier on duty at the club for details about the Italian sailors arrested in Palestine.

"Why do you want to know?" the soldier asked.

"One of them is a kinsman," explained Mario. "I want to know how he's getting along."

The soldier went off to report that a suspicious character was hanging around the club and asking questions. He was instructed to direct Mario to the rabbi of Milan's Jewish community. Mario went there, followed at a distance by two of our men to see what he was really up to.

Mario told the astounded rabbi about his keen desire to join the operation of smuggling Jews. The rabbi refused to do anything, and reported the conversation to us. We were sure that Mario was a British agent. Nevertheless, it was decided to establish contact with him in order to get to his superiors. Our men quickly discovered, however, that Mario was on the level, and that he was indeed a skilled seaman. He earned their confidence, was given command of the blockade-runner *Wingate,* and was captured aboard the ship near the coast of Eretz-Yisrael.

Among the other Italians, the most outstanding was Ricardo, Mario's mate. About thirty, tall and broad-shouldered, with coal-black hair and an impressive mustache, he would have seemed at home on a Hollywood set or the stage of an Italian opera. He was quite reticent. Like Mario, he had served aboard an Italian submarine and knew the sea. He could be trusted.

Damini, the *Wingate's* engineer, impressed us immediately with his knowledge of things technical. Our favorite, however, was Gino, a youth of nineteen, a native of Fiume, half-Italian, half-Yugoslav. Our cause captured Gino's young heart. He was thrilled with the adventure and admired the rugged Palyam men.

Among the other seamen on the *Enzo Sereni* were two remarkable old sailors. One was thin and long-nosed and generally resembled an ancient rooster. The other, about seventy, went about with a square, expressionless Boris Karloff face. The *Enzo* engineer, Pescatti, also proved to be a skillful and trustworthy mechanic. Gigino, the boatswain, was at first put out because Mario had been ranked above him, but since he was not particularly astute, it was a simple matter for the shrewd Mario to overcome his resentment.

Limassol

THE NIGHT passed quickly in the cove. At dawn the sea appeared to have calmed down quite a bit, and I urged Yaacov to get under way. We were already a day behind schedule. At five in the morning we weighed anchor and headed out to sea, but half an hour in the rough waters convinced us that we had best seek shelter again. At eight we reached another cove. Not far away we saw a sailing vessel which had also put into the cove because of the high seas. A small boat was being lowered from that ship, and all our men immediately went down into the hold. In the boat were the master of the vessel and a boy. The master was a fat old Syrian, come to exchange some gossip with Yaacov over a friendly cup of Turkish coffee. The two sat together for about an hour sipping coffee, and the Syrian went back to his own craft. Our men remained below until nightfall. Again we enjoyed a tranquil night in the cove, but we chafed at the thought that we had already lost two precious days.

Mario and the Palyam men went over the *Ada* and decided that due to her overall instability it would be most risky to sail directly to Crete and thence to the Adriatic. We would have to hug the shoreline, where we might find quick shelter from storm. Our timetable was becoming increasingly upset.

The next day the sea was calm and we sailed in a north westerly direction, most of us lounging in the bows and relaxing. About ten o'clock the *Ada* slowed down and soon came to a halt.

"What's up?" I shouted to Yaacov.

He hesitated. "Everything's all right," he finally said. "A bit of motor trouble. I'm sending the engineer down."

But when Yacoub, the engineer, came up from the engine room about half an hour later, we still had no answer. He couldn't locate the trouble. Yaacov favored him with a string of curses and went below himself. Soon he too returned, none the wiser. I asked Mario to have his engineers, Pescatti and Damini, go down and take a look. We were sick with apprehension. They came back dragging the shaft which connected the motor with the screw. They laid the shaft on the deck and examined it, as we watched with mounting anxiety. Finally they gave their verdict:

"Shaft is broken."

We were stunned. It took a few moments for the words to sink in. I called a council of war. Yaacov went to pieces, raving and ranting, cursing himself and the boat, bewailing the day he had made the deal with us. We realized that only a repair job on shore could restore the *Ada* to service. We still had sail, but this method of propulsion would take sixty days to get us to Italy, not six.

The port of Paphos, the *Ada's* official destination, lay to the north. The nearest port with machine-shop facilities was Limassol. Any captain overtaken with such a mishap while on the way to Paphos would head for Limassol for repairs. With heavy hearts we decided to backtrack and make our way there. But the *Ada* did not handle well under sail. We tacked back and forth, port and starboard, until the wind finally caught a corner of the sail and sent the craft creeping toward Limassol. We drifted along for the better part of a day. Near Limassol we all went down into the hold, leaving only Yaacov and his crew on deck. Abdullah and Abed covered the hold with planks and tarpaulins and nailed them down. We were gambling that the customs officials would not ask to have the hatch opened if told that the hold was empty. Below, we were prepared for just such an emergency: iron rations, water and chamber pots. A hole bored in the wall between hold and forecastle kept us in communication with the ship's crew.

Toward evening the *Ada* made port and cast anchor. Yaacov came to the hole in the forecastle with a nervous whisper: a British police launch was anchored no more than an oar's length away. We spent a horrible night. The air was foul. The old Italians relieved themselves every hour. In the morning Yaacov went into the town with the broken shaft, promising to return by noon.

The hours dragged on. The stench mounted. Our appetites were gone, and so were our spirits. Some of the Italians whiled away the time at cards in the faint light which came filtering through the cracks in the deck. We had to caution them again and again as they forgot where they were and raised their voices in the heat of the game. The others were more troublesome, especially the two old men, to whose groaning there was no end. The Boris Karloff character lay in a half-faint. His companion kept coughing and spitting. By afternoon some of the sailors were near mutiny.

"Why do we have to be cooped up here, suffocating like this?"

Mario was able to calm them somewhat. Now it was evening, and Yaacov had still not returned. The Italians were in a rage. Even Mario was despondent and lay motionless. In defiance of the orders I had given Yaacov, Yacoub and Abdullah left the vessel and headed for the brothels in the port. Only little Abed was left, our sole contact with the world outside. Darkness fell. We decided that if Yaacov wasn't back in half an hour, I would go and look for him. I would take his uniform, wrap it in oilskins, swim to shore, put on the uniform and hunt for him, or perhaps make contact with some Jews.

But Yaacov now showed up in a rowboat with Abdullah. Why hadn't he been in touch with us all day? Better that we shouldn't ask. His hair was turning white from all the grief we had caused him. He was a bundle of nerves. As for the broken shaft, repairs would be made that night. Mario passed the information on to the mutinous Italians.

At ten, Yaacov went back ashore and returned at midnight with the shaft, welded and repaired. The Italian engineers set about installing it. Shortly after midnight they started the motor and announced that it was functioning properly; we could put out to sea. We weighed anchor and slipped out of the harbor. The men burst out on deck for some fresh air. We were free. The Italians broke into song. The night was starlit, clear and cold. The vessel skimmed the waves like a seagull. Toward dawn we fell asleep, worn out but calm.

We awakened late in the morning. Everything seemed to be in good order. Our men gathered in the bows and chatted. Some of the Italians went back to their cards. Suddenly the motor stopped and the vessel came to a halt. The Italian engineers dived for the engine room. Soon they were back. The shaft was broken—this time in two places.

Yaacov flew into a rage and cursed the day he was born. I sat down with the Palyam men to plan a course of action. We agreed that we couldn't return to Limassol. The repair job would take days and we couldn't keep the men cooped up that long, nor could we run the risk of being detected by the British. We considered going back to our own country under sail, stealing ashore past the destroyers, and beginning all over again. The British, however, would in all likelihood capture us. Wouldn't it be better to chance the unknown than to retrace our course? It was unanimously decided to head north and sail for Turkey, beyond British reach. We would rather be imprisoned by the Turks than by the British, if it came to that. We would cast anchor in a Turkish port and claim to be refugees who had been aboard a blockade-running vessel which had foundered in a storm and who were picked up by the *Ada*. We would ask the Turkish authorities for help. We might even succeed in making contact with our home headquarters and with the men of our branch in Istanbul. We hoisted sail and waited for a wind. Of course, the wind was down to a faint breeze. Slowly the *Ada* glided forward. We passed Cape Arnauti, at the north western corner of Cyprus. The shores of the island gradually receded. Another day passed. We were now close to Turkey and knew that once we reached its coast we would be at the mercy of the winds. We felt like those ancient mariners who sailed into the unknown and gave themselves up to the mighty forces of nature. If an east wind came up, we would sail toward Marsina and anchor there.

The following morning we saw the lofty mountains of Anatolia and reached the vicinity of Cape Anamur. A west wind was blowing, and we were driven east. We sailed slowly along the beautiful coast of Turkey, where rugged mountains, covered with green, sloped steeply to a narrow beach. Frequently there was not even a beach. All we could see were boulders, against which the waves crashed mightily. Here and there we spotted small villages. These were not marked on our "marvelous" map, but Abdullah could tell us something about each one.

On the fourth day the wind shifted, and we drifted west. Our food supplies were running low, as was our patience. We decided to put in at the nearest port, come what may. We scanned the map. Abdullah and Yaacov activated their memories. We finally located a small port town west of Marsina—Silipca. We sailed another day and got to within twenty miles of Silipca. But again the wind failed us. Next morning we were still at the same spot, becalmed.

The "Bodrum"

THE MORNING was bright and clear, the sea calm. Fabi pointed to a small dot on the eastern horizon. The field-glasses revealed a small vessel flying the Turkish flag. Soon we could hear the gay clatter of its motor. I ordered the Turkish flag to be hoisted and an S.O.S. signalled. We waved the semaphore flags, flapped our arms, flashed mirrors, until we succeeded in attracting the attention of the crew on the approaching vessel. Our men again went below. Abdullah, who spoke Turkish, Yaacov and I stayed on deck. Our intention was to ask the Turks to tow us, for a fee, to Silipca. The Turkish vessel, with its ornately carved prow, drew near, and a tall Turk, wearing a knitted cap, hailed us. Abdullah explained that our motor had broken down and we needed a tow to Silipca. The Turk wanted to know how much and in what currency we would pay. Guessing that paper bills would not persuade him, I instructed Abdullah to offer him gold. Fifty sovereigns, demanded the Turk. No, thanks, much obliged. The Turk sailed away.

Soon, however, he reversed course and approached us again. He had smelled money and was hooked. We decided to ask him to tow us not east to Silipca but west along the Turkish coast. There was also no point in concealing from him the presence of men aboard. We would do better to tell him they were shipwrecked sailors.

The Turk came to a stop about fifty yards away, lowered a small boat and drew near. We put a rope ladder over the side and took him into Yaacov's cabin. Over a cup of coffee we had a friendly chat. It turned out that he could speak broken Italian and could therefore converse with Mario, who told him we had some Italian and Austrian sailors aboard who had been members of the crew of an Italian freighter, the *Dori,* plying between Egypt and Italy. The *Dori* had gone down in a storm a few days previously, and the survivors had been picked up by the *Ada,* whose motor was disabled in the same storm. "Needless to say," added Mario piously, "all the survivors are praying to get back to their homes."

We led the Turk out on deck so that he could peer into the hold and see the miserable "survivors" with his own eyes. His home port was Bodrum, in western Anatolia, opposite the Greek island of Kos, and *Bodrum* was also the name of his ship. His regular run was between Anatolia and Alexandretta. On this trip he had taken cargo to Silipca and was going home in ballast.

Now we made a new suggestion. Instead of towing us to Bodrum, why not transfer us to his vessel and drop us off at Kos? The island was only a short distance from Bodrum, and so he would be making no sacrifice. This was a daring offer, but the Turk went along. How much would we pay? After some bargaining, we finally settled for thirty gold sovereigns. While the bargaining was at its height I took out a dozen heavy, glittering gold coins and jingled them suggestively in the palm of my hand. The Turk's eyes almost popped out of his head. When I offered him ten sovereigns as an advance, to be paid when we boarded his vessel, the deal was closed without further discussion.

It was not until all our men were actually aboard the *Bodrum,* together with our fuel and water tanks, equipment and food supplies, that I felt safe. I knew that if worst came to worst we outnumbered the others on board and could take control. The Turk demanded from Yaacov a certified statement about the sinking of the *Dori.* I went into Yaacov's cabin and penned a heart-rending statement in English about the last days of the ill-starred *Dori,* which I signed in bold letters: "Patriarch Abraham, Captain." The Turk picked up the document, examined it from all angles and shoved it in his pocket. I could see that he was delighted.

Before saying good-bye to Yaacov, I begged him to let our people back home know about us as soon as he reached a Turkish port.

The *Bodrum* got under way, and we stood on deck wondering at the unforeseen twist in our fortunes. The *Ada* soon disappeared from sight.

The *Bodrum* was a fine-looking ship, and unlike the *Ada* was expertly handled. She was painted red, green and blue in the imaginative Turkish tradition; she was scrubbed clean from stem to stern. Her capacity was about forty tons, and she was propelled by well-tended sails on two tall masts and by an ancient German motor. Her owners were two brothers named Musloom. One of them, the tall Turk with whom we had dealt, was the captain, a man of about forty, with the face of a bewhiskered buccaneer. A knitted cap permanently draped his forehead. He had a set of buck teeth, some of them gold and others steel. His partner-brother was not a seaman. About seventy, he was taciturn and sour-tempered, with a wrinkled face to match.

There were three other seamen aboard: the engineer, in his twenties, with Mongolian features—agile, muscular, the kind you would expect to come upon brandishing a knife; an old Cretan whose life had been spent in Turkish ships; and the captain's son, a rotund and phlegmatic boy of about fifteen.

We informed the captain that I was the leader of the "non-Italian" contingent, which he had already guessed. This earned me an invitation to sleep in the captain's cabin. We arranged matters as we did on the *Ada*. I shared the captain's quarters in the stern, our men were in the main hold, and the Turks were in the forecastle. The *Bodrum* hold was cleaner and more spacious than that of the *Ada*. Musloom's cabin had two bunks, spread with goatskins and woollen blankets. The walls were adorned with quotations from the Koran and with other decorations.

The helm, in the stern, was worthy of display in a marine museum. The compass had evidently served generations of navigators. I asked Musloom to allow our men as well as his to take the helm, and he agreed.

We sailed toward Adalia Bay. The sea was tranquil, mirror-smooth. The *Bodrum* sliced through the water like a hot knife through butter.

The first evening we threw a party. We had some canned meat and some noodles. The Italians, in excellent spirits, cooked macaroni. The *Bodrum* had a primus stove, something the *Ada* lacked. Now we could have hot meals. The Turks prepared spicy Eastern dishes, and each group invited the other to partake of its culinary triumph. Captain Musloom produced some bottles of mastika—a potent Turkish anise-flavored liquor—and passed them around. The cabin-boy served Turkish coffee. The Italians, never the ones to miss such an opportunity, serenaded us with sea chanteys, *solo* and *tutti,* a medley of patriotic tunes, and sentimental, romantic ballads. Our men contributed their share. Even the brooding Turks laughed and clapped their hands.

Somehow it suddenly dawned on the Turk that he was dealing with "Israelites." The light began to come when, little by little, we let him know that our intention was to reach Italy. First we said that we would rather have him drop us off not at Kos but at Samos, west of Kos, in return—naturally—for a few more gold coins. Then we asked him to take us to Sephanos, shifting our destination westward, until he realized that we wanted to reach Italy, not Greece.

The next day we laid plans to seize the vessel, if the Turk tried to hand us over to the authorities. Our men were in control of the helm; the course had been charted jointly by Musloom and Mario on our old German map. Our men were positioned in such a way that every Turk aboard had two of us watching him. "Churchill" and Gino were assigned to keep an eye on the captain, the strongest of the lot.

After four days of travel, the Turks realized that we were determined to reach Italy. The captain now decided that he would show me who was boss. At noon of the fifth day, as I entered the cabin, he was elaborately cleaning an old rusty German musket which he had fished out of the heavy sea-chest next to his bunk. From a cloth sack he exhumed some bullets which he began to clean and polish. (I recalled Jack London's description of the cook in *The Sea Wolf* sitting and honing his knife hour after hour in order to intimidate his antagonist.) Musloom then strode out on deck, girded with bullets and carrying his loaded gun, and began sharpening his aim by taking pot-shots at pieces of paper he threw overboard.

We decided to launch a counterattack. That evening, as Mario and I sat in Musloom's cabin, I casually opened our first-aid chest and began arranging the individual bandages, which had been rolled up and enclosed in small cylinders. Mario kept warning me to handle the dynamite gently. I attempted to reassure him, and the two of us kept batting words like "gelignite" and "dynamite" back and forth. This verbal barrage unnerved the Turk completely. Next morning I found the revolver lying on my bed. Musloom informed me, via Mario, that he had full confidence in me and as a token was leaving the gun and bullets in my care. This ended the cold war between the Turks and ourselves. They knew—and by this time we were in the Straits of Rhodes—that nothing would deter us from setting our course for Italy.

Coming into the Straits, we again took all the necessary precautions. The men went down into the hold. The *Bodrum* passed Rhodes with her Turkish flag flapping jauntily in the wind. We passed a British destroyer and saluted it with due international courtesy.

Half an hour later we found ourselves in the middle of a Royal Navy flotilla of mine-sweepers. The Turks ceremoniously saluted each of the vessels, and were highly pleased to be saluted in return.

The *Bodrum* was now but a day's distance from her home port. We opened final negotiations with the Turks. Mario and I told the brothers that if they took us to Italy they would be rewarded with a fortune. I offered to give them forty pieces of gold on the spot, plus one hundred and ten more once we reached Italy—a total of one hundred and fifty. The brothers conferred at great length before acquiescing. It was agreed that the older Musloom would go ashore with the money in the evening, while we would continue on to Italy.

Toward evening, however, as we sailed along the green Anatolian coast, we sensed that all was not well. The Muslooms were huddling together, and the Turkish sailors were also summoned to conference. After supper Captain Musloom announced that he could not take us to Italy. He would drop us off at Kos that same night or the next day. He explained that in the first place, he had no papers for Italy. Even if he were to land us there safely, he himself might be arrested and fined in Turkey for leaving without certification. Moreover, the vessel didn't have enough food, water or fuel to reach Italy. Finally, though he himself could be persuaded to go along with our request, his older brother was against it, wishing to avoid any adventure that might endanger the boat.

We tried hard to persuade the Turks, but could not budge them. We talked to them for hours. We promised the captain that once in Italy we would hire a car and show him the country in all its beauty. Mario promised him other pleasures in abundant measure. He described the charms of the Italian women, down to the last detail. We told him about the high positions we enjoyed in Italy; why, we were held in esteem in every harbor! We could get him trade between Turkey and Italy. But the old Turk wouldn't listen.

I decided to put an end to the fruitless negotiations. Mario and I went out on deck and I held a conference with our men. We could easily seize the boat and take it to Italy, but this would be piracy. Moreover, if we were forced by a storm or for other reasons to enter a Greek or Turkish port, we would face severe punishment for appropriating a vessel, a serious crime. Food and water were running low, and the fuel supply wouldn't hold out. We would have to put in at some port and replenish our supplies before we reached our destination, Termoli.

By this time, of course, the whole Termoli plan appeared highly dubious. Back home we were told that a Mossad man would wait for us in Termoli a few days, beginning with the sixth day after our departure. Now that so much time had elapsed, the man had probably given up and gone.

We told the Turks that we agreed to their putting in at their home port for a permit to sail from Bodrum to Italy. They jumped for joy. Captain Musloom swore by the beard of the Prophet that no harm would come to us in his native town. All the dignitaries were his bosom friends. The permit would be forthcoming without any trouble, and we would be on our way to Italy in no time at all. Bottles of mastika were produced to celebrate the "new agreement." We contributed our last bottle of brandy and clinked glasses to toast "brotherhood and companionship." At midnight we handed the helm over to Musloom, and he guided the ship expertly right up to the pier.

At dawn we beheld Bodrum, a small Turkish port town half-hidden in the arms which formed the bay. It was surrounded by walls and fortifications built in bygone days. It had served the Crusaders as an embarkation port for the Holy Land and later, in the Middle Ages, was on the route of the Italian merchantmen.

Again we went down into the hold—"miserable seamen, survivors of a shipwreck." We had no need for make-up costumes. Our natural appearance was convincing enough—tattered, dirty, bearded, draped in filthy blankets. Our cover story was the same: we were seamen; Mario was our captain; our men were natives of Yugoslavia, Czechoslovakia and Austria. We hoped that Bodrum's officials were not conversant with these languages.

The Musiooms left the boat and went into town. We remained below, waiting. Soon the captain came back with the *kaimakam*, the town's police officer, a stocky man in a well-pressed gray uniform adorned with red shoulderbands studded with gilt stars. He wore a stiff Prussian-like helmet and highly-polished black boots. The *kaimakam* stood on the deck, feet apart and arms folded, a veritable Napoleon. He looked down at us and said not a word. After a long and oppressive silence, he began a lengthy interrogation. Mario, officially our captain, also served as an interpreter. He asked that the *Bodrum* be permitted to take us to Italy.

Other officers, policemen and soldiers gathered about, some on duty and others out of sheer curiosity. A town like Bodrum did not get to see shipwrecked Italian sailors every day. We were the center of attraction. The officers noted down our names and addresses, posted an armed guard and left. The Muslooms went home.

We were now the wards of the *kaimakam*. As we no longer had to maintain our bedraggled look, we washed, shaved and came up on deck to enjoy the sight of the town and the Crusader ruins at the mouth of the bay. About noon, the *kaimakam* returned. His answer was disappointing. We would not be allowed to continue on our way. The matter, he claimed, was outside his jurisdiction, and he would have to submit it to Izmir. Meanwhile, we were under arrest. He turned on his heel and marched pompously away.

It was possible that the *kaimakam's* grandiloquence meant that he wanted a bribe. But what kind of bribe could do him justice? Gold? Yes, but our gold was to go to the Muslooms. Our dollars and lire were for the food and fuel we would need. But we had a splendid alternative—watches. Specifically, the ornate stop-watches which Bezalel and I had bought in Haifa for our comrades, the anti-magnetic watches with the luminous dials and compasses. Irresistible! We decided to sacrifice one of these magnificent watches on the altar of the Great God Bribery.

When Musloom returned at dusk his usually sour face was wreathed in benign smiles. He was a bundle of joy, for that was what his wife had just given him—a male offspring! Musloom would now have to stay away from his wife for a while, and he was only human. He recalled Mario's vivid description of Italy's robust beauties. He was now ready to sail with us. He assured us that bribes presented to the *kaimakam* and the local customs officer would sweep away all the obstacles. Good-bye, two watches.

Musloom was right, of course. Toward evening the *kaimakam* appeared and graciously condescended to accept our modest but cordial gift. The extraordinary watch enthralled him. Next came His Honor, the Customs Officer. We urged him in the name of brotherhood to accept this small souvenir of our visit. He took it and said he was impressed by our sincere good wishes. Much to our chagrin, these two worthies were followed by half a dozen others, each sporting a resounding title and stars to match. We bade a fond adieu to all the timepieces. I am sure that to this day accurate time is determined in Bodrum according to those watches of ours.

Musloom brought a merchant, who, in return for the rest of our money, agreed to stock us with food, water and fuel. Next morning

I was summoned to the office of the *kaimakam*. I was requested to sign an agreement, written in Turkish, obligating me as the treasurer of our group to pay the Honorable Captain Musloom the sum of one hundred and ten English gold coins upon our reaching Brindisi in Italy. I signed the document formally: "Captain Lookforme." Musloom and the *kaimakam* affixed about a dozen enormous Turkish stamps to the document. Everything was now perfectly legal. I gave Musloom his advance of gold coins and we prepared to sail. Suddenly the elder brother appeared. The old boy wanted to share in the profit and perhaps in the amorous charms of the Italian beauties. We weighed anchor.

The Turk stopped at a deserted beach a few miles from town. He was an infinitely better seaman than Yaacov of the *Ada*. He saw to it that his vessel was in proper ballast before setting out for the open sea. All of us went ashore, filled sacks with gravel and emptied them into the hold. The *Bodrum* now had adequate ballast. We sailed slowly among the islands of the Aegean, passing Kos, Leros, Samos and scores of other isles scattered like dark green patches on the deep blue sea between Anatolia and the shores of Greece. Two days passed quietly and pleasantly.

The third day out we ran into a storm which tossed the poor *Bodrum* like a driven leaf. Musloom had never been outside Turkish waters. He had no faith in this sea and in these strange shores. As the storm grew wilder, he handed the vessel over to Mario and secluded himself in his cabin. His older brother fell to his knees, weeping and praying.

For two days we were tossed from one island to another. On the third day we put in at a small inlet on Sephanos Island. We waited two days for the storm to subside, then continued westward. We debated whether to shorten our route by going through the Corinth Canal or to sail around Cape Matapan. We weren't sure if the Canal was open to traffic following the damage done there by the Germans during the war. We were also apprehensive about possible British patrols. We decided to circle the Pelopennesian Peninsula. Near Cape Matapan we stopped for half a day to rehabilitate our aged motor, and our excellent Italian engineers were able to restore it to life.

Three more days passed as we sailed along the western coast of Greece. Again we were overtaken by a storm. The motor coughed consumptively. We looked for shelter. We were near Cephalonia

Island, and found a hidden cove, like a fjord, beneath overhanging cliffs. We sailed in and followed it to the end. The water was perfectly calm. We lowered anchor and went ashore, where we began to forage for food with which to replenish our supplies.

After an hour's walk, we saw a solitary farmhouse and went in. It was empty, but we found the family in the field, harvesting the sparse wheat with scythes—a wrinkled old Greek farmer, his son and two granddaughters. We told them that we were Italian sailors seeking shelter from the storm. In broken Italian he told us about the horrible German occupation of the island during the war. Most of the inhabitants had either fled or been killed. We offered him a can of preserves for some chickens, and he agreed. We helped his pretty granddaughters capture the chickens, and in the evening we went down to the beach with the girls and had a cook-out. The Italians began dancing, and we followed with a *hora* which swept up the Italians and the young Greek girls.

At dawn we set sail northward.

Gallipoli

THE NEARER we drew to the tip of the Italian boot, the more we were bothered by the problem of where to land. We would obviously be arrested as soon as we put in at any port. Our tiny Turkish craft would arouse suspicion by its mere presence in an Italian port. The Italian sailors had no documents, to say nothing of our own men.

How could we disembark without being caught? How were we to make contact with our people in Italy? Our fuel was giving out, and we could not reach Termoli. To make matters worse, none of the Italian sailors was a native of the south. The only ones they knew in the southern ports were the prostitutes. Sailors and prostitutes always seem to defy the limitations of geography.

We finally decided on Gallipoli, on the southeastern shore of the Gulf of Taranto. Perhaps this small town was not closely supervised by port police and customs officials. More important was the fact that our sailors had two familiar addresses there. We would enter Gallipoli under cover of darkness, go ashore, and get settled in a brothel until we could get in touch with our people in the north. We told the Turk that he would be paid as soon as we got the money from our people in Italy.

We approached the port of Gallipoli at dusk. Surreptitiously we joined a fleet of fishing smacks on their way back to port. Our entry was smooth and flawless. We maintained strict silence. Most of the men went below. We asked the Turk not to issue orders in his own language. Musloom became suspicious; we had told him that scores of friends were waiting for us in Italy. He began to rant and rave. Mario was able to calm him down and to get him and his men down into the hold. We pulled up at the quiet pier along with the returning fishermen, but to be on the safe side, we did not tie up. We sent Damini ashore in a skiff to explore the situation. We were tense and silent—except for Musloom. He kept yelling and cursing at the top of his voice. We warned him that if he didn't shut up, he would be arrested. Then we told him that we were going to leave the boat. He was dumbfounded, but Mario promised him that he, Mario, would remain behind as a hostage, and that all our luggage would stay aboard. The next day, God willing, we would return and double his emolument. The Turk fell silent and remained in his cabin. His older brother kept up a continuous moaning.

Damini returned an hour later, having arranged with the madam of a brothel to accept about a dozen men. He had also had a word with Lucia, a self-employed prostitute recommended by Mario, who agreed to put up six guests. We split up into threes—two Italians and one of our men. I went first, with Damini and Gino. The two Italians chatted loudly, while I came through with an occasional *si, si.* We passed a bored policeman at the pier and turned our steps toward town.

Gallipoli is an ancient town, with narrow streets and old houses huddled together, seemingly on the verge of collapsing. We walked along the streets and alleys until we reached the brothel. We knocked on the heavy iron door. A fat old madam, heavily made up, dressed in an old bathrobe and decked out with cheap jewelry, greeted us with a broad and ringing *buona sera.* Damini pointed to me and said that I had a severe headache—could I have a separate room? The old lady led the way to a tiny room in the attic. The furnishings were standard: a large, dirty bed, a filthy sink, a cracked mirror and a picture of the Virgin above the bed. Fifteen minutes later came the next trio, until we had a full house—a dozen Italians, Menahem and I.

Damini returned from Lucia's past midnight with the news that everything was fine. Four of our men and two Italians were all sleeping across Lucia's wide bed. Mario and the Turks remained aboard the vessel. The plan called for Mario to get in touch with the Mossad men in the early morning and ask them to send a sum of money to a bank in Gallipoli for him. When the money arrived, we would pay the Turk, hire a car and leave Gallipoli.

I was up at six. I peered through the window shutters and saw two or three policemen loitering in front of the door, as well as a couple of men in mufti, obviously detectives. I awakened Menahem, and a few minutes later Damini burst into the room, highly agitated.

"The house is surrounded by police."

We were trapped. I ran quickly down to the main room on the

first floor, where the Italians had assembled. I tried to calm them. They could not be accused of any serious crime. After all, they *were* Italians, albeit without identification cards. Our case was different—we were foreigners. I asked them to give themselves up to the police without protest or resistance, but not to reveal the presence of others in the house. They were sure to be interrogated, and I asked them not to give any hint of us or of our mission. Then I went back to the attic. We locked the door on the inside and closed the shutters, hoping that the mass surrender of the Italians would deter the police from searching the house.

Damini and his genial companions had overlooked a simple fact. Most of the madams who operated brothels tended to cooperate with the police. As soon as we fell asleep, apparently, our hostess ran to the police and informed them that a band of suspicious characters, including two Germans, had come to her place for shelter.

Groups of Fascists and Nazi deserters still roamed southern Italy, hiding from the Allies. Aided by smugglers, these groups set up escape routes from the southern ports to Spain and thence to Latin America. Our blond hair and blue eyes were enough to make the madam believe that Menahem and I were Aryans.

The local police were hesitant about dealing alone with such dangerous adversaries, which was why we hadn't been arrested during the night. They got in touch with Lecce, the county seat, and asked for instructions. The police commandant in Lecce ordered the house to be surrounded at once. He also got in touch with Bari and asked that the FSS (British Army Field Security Service) take a hand.

Menahem and I decided to hide under the bed and wait. Before crawling under the rickety contraption, I went back and unlocked the door, so as not to tempt fate. We lay there and heard the police burst into the house. Apparently taken aback by the docile group they found, they merely swung open the doors of the other rooms, including ours, and shut them with the call of *niente*, "nothing."

I peered through the shutters. Our Italians, handcuffed, were being herded into a truck. A moment later the neighborhood was quiet.

What about our comrades at Lucia's, we wondered. Had they, too, been arrested? Mario and the Turks were probably in chains. Luckily, I had asked Damini for Lucia's address. I had it, written down: Via Battisti 12.

Lucia

WE REMAINED in our room until dark, spelling each other at the window. The detectives, after a few perfunctory march-pasts, went away. With darkness, we slipped out of the house and melted into the alleys. Some children were playing in the street. "Where is Via Battisti?" I asked.

They were silent, frightened, and we hurried away. We were afraid to ask adults, who might become suspicious and alert the police. All at once we found ourselves being followed by a young lad, who began to nag us for cigarettes. We promised him three cigarettes if he would direct us to Via Battisti. We followed him for about fifteen minutes, and finally reached the house we wanted. We descended several steps to a cellar, then continued past garbage cans, dirty infants and wash hung out on a line. A young woman was sitting on the steps, nursing a baby. She glanced at us, pointed to a door and said, in a dead voice: "Lucia."

We knocked. A young woman appeared at the door. She was of medium height, dark-skinned, with black hair and almond-shaped eyes. A short, faded dress emphasized the charms of her rounded figure. She looked at us in fear and asked what we wanted. I tried to tell her, in my broken Italian, that we were looking for some friends. She shook her head stubbornly: "Not here!"

Our disappointment was unmistakable. At least, when Lucia spoke up again, her voice was friendlier. She fished out a piece of paper and handed it to us: "Write your names."

I wrote the code names we had been given back home. At Lucia's call a young girl came to the door. She took the paper, listened to Lucia's whispered orders, and disappeared. When she came back a good five minutes later, her face was all smiles: *Va bene* ("All's well.")

We were still in the dark. Where were the others? Lucia led us to her room and up a steep staircase to the roof. We jumped across to the next roof and descended to a yard, crossed a jungle of courtyards and climbed up to another roof. Lucia knocked at a small door and called out her own name. The door opened. We found ourselves in a fairly large room illuminated by a solitary lamp. We hardly had time to look around when Fabi, Uri, Haim, Bezalel and the two Italians assailed us with frenzied handshakes and back-slappings. Our friends, it seemed, had the same experience that we did. They fell asleep in Lucia's house but were awakened when she came to warn them that they might be arrested at any moment. She had already heard that the others had been detained. The two Italians begged her to help, for there was nowhere all of them could flee, and she arranged this hideaway in the home of fishermen friends.

Eventually the police did knock on Lucia's door.

"You had clients last night?"

"Yes."

"How many?"

"Six."

"Any foreigners?"

"Yes, four."

"How long were they with you?"

"All night. They left in the morning."

"Where did they go?"

"I don't know. I don't ask my clients where they go."

The police gave up and left.

I examined the room where my comrades had found refuge. It obviously served the fisherman's family as a combined living-room, dining-room and storeroom. The family now stood around us, gazing at us with curiosity and compassion.

I suddenly felt hungry. We had not eaten all day The old *signora,* with the help of her daughters and Lucia, prepared a royal repast for Menahem and me: heaps of fried fish, bread and a jug of *vino rosso*. The *signora* pressed us to eat and drink. Out came more fish and more jugs. But all we could give in return was our humble thanks; our pockets were empty.

Lucia told us that the town was swarming with security men searching for the eight strangers as yet unaccounted for—according to Musloom's reckoning. The Turk had told the police everything he knew. British Army intelligence was also taking a hand, and the entire town was in an uproar. We realized that sooner or later we were bound to be caught if we lingered, and that we had to find some avenue of escape. But where, and how?

We asked Lucia whether there were any Jews in Gallipoli. No, none in Gallipoli, but there were many not far from the town. The fishermen broke in to explain that there were *campi ebrei* in Santa Maria and Santa Crozza, about ten miles away.

This was quite a piece of information. I suddenly recalled that back home I had read reports mentioning the proposed establishment of large camps for thousands of refugees in the Gallipoli area. Excited, we asked Lucia whether it would be possible to get a letter through to those camps that very night. She consulted with the fisherman's family. Yes, the fishermen would be going out after midnight, and they were prepared to take the letter.

We wrote it in three languages—Hebrew, Yiddish and English. But on second thought we decided that such a letter would not do. What Jew would put stock in such a letter, delivered in the dead of night by an Italian fisherman? The best and shortest way was to get to the camps ourselves. Would the fishermen agree to take us there?

They did, without hesitation. We took off our shoes and put on fishermen's shirts, and each of us picked up a net. There was still some time before midnight. We sat around in that pleasant atmosphere, with Lucia and her pretty eight-year-old daughter Anna and the fisherman's family. Anna's head was on Menahem's lap, and he sang Hebrew lullabies to her.

We left the house in pairs about half an hour after midnight—the old father and I, one of the sons and Fabi, another son and Uri. We shuffled along the streets of Gallipoli in the faint moonlight. A few *carabinieri* patrolled the streets. Barefoot, we passed right by them, half-hidden under the nets after the manner of Gallipoli fishermen on their way to fish with lanterns.

As soon as we came back to the beach we hid among the rocks, while the two sons went back for the others. The father went to get the boat. Shortly after one o'clock we were all aboard. The fishermen's hands, powerful and experienced, grasped the oars, and the boat sped westward over the calm water along the shoreline. From time to time we spelled the fishermen at the oars. Suddenly one of them pointed to a ray of light on the shore ahead. *"Campo ebreo!"* We glided to the shore, got out and hid again among some rocks. I asked the youngest of the fishermen to check the source of the light.

It was now four in the morning. Our teeth chattered with the cold. After a long wait, the fisherman came back with the information: the light was coming from the house of the *polizia ebrea,* the Jewish police headquarters. After all our wanderings, this seemed too good to be true.

I now wanted to explore the situation myself. I asked my companions to wait and went ahead with the fisherman. I saw an ordinary sentry box, illuminated with a "lux" lamp. Near it stood a burly fellow in khaki. An armband bearing a Star of David read "Camp Police." I approached and said, somewhat emotionally: *"Shalom aleichem."*

He looked at me in surprise but made no reply. I suddenly thought about my appearance—dirty, unshaven, barefoot, my head topped with the shapeless straw hat of an Italian fisherman. I tried again, this time with more gladness in my voice: *"Shalom aleichem,* friend!"

The sentry suddenly came to life.

"Go back to your tent and sleep!" he shouted. "You drunken bum! I'll arrest you, filthy pig! You have nothing to do but run to Gallipoli and get drunk and sell your shoes for wine! To your tent!"

"Listen, friend," I pleaded. "I and a few other fellows came here from Eretz-Yisrael to work in the refugee camps. We're in trouble. We need help."

He came closer. "How did you get here from Eretz-Yisrael?"

"In a boat."

"So, in a boat," he exclaimed, staring at me. "In a boat, from Eretz-Yisrael?"

"That's right—in a boat, from Eretz-Yisrael."

The sentry lost all control. "Either you go to your tent, you lying drunkard, or I'll arrest you on the spot!"

"Listen, friend," I said, "I am ready to have you arrest me, but first I want you to get the head guard here."

The sentry put me into the guardhouse and went to call his superior. As soon as I saw the man I felt that I would be able to get through to him. He was a young fellow, but he had the look of an old soldier about him. I repeated my story. He heard me out, didn't hesitate a moment, and sent a few men from the night-watch to get my companions. At the same time, he called together an emergency meeting of the "Aliya Groups" committee in the camp.

At five in the morning, then, I was chairing a session of the five committee members—two "Noham" groups and one each of the

"Hashomer Hatzair," "Betar" and "Zionist Youth." At six the first messengers left for Bari, Naples and Rome to acquaint the Mossad people with our plight and to summon emergency aid. The news spread throughout the camp like wildfire: Jewish soldiers had come from Eretz-Yisrael to organize the *aliya!*

In the morning, after a short sleep and even before I got through to the Italian branch, I asked the camp commander to send a courier to Gallipoli. He returned toward evening and reported that the Italian sailors and the Turks were in the local jail. Lucia had agreed to look after them.

The next day an American army truck bearing markings of the Joint Distribution Committee arrived at the camp. The driver identified himself as the Mossad man in Bari. He had orders from "Alon" (Yehuda Arazi, head of the Italian branch) to bring our men and the two Italians north. I was to remain in the Santa Maria camp and see to the welfare of the prisoners in Gallipoli.

For three days I moved about and made friends with the excited people in the camp. Meanwhile, Lucia was looking after the men in jail, bringing them hot food and laundering their clothes. I told the courier to assure her that she would be paid.

On the morning of the fourth day a green pick-up truck with UNRRA insignia drove into the camp. The driver, Avram, was a young lad from one of our settlements, with a wide grin and tousled hair. He had orders to drive me to Mossad headquarters in Milan. I took leave of my hosts and we drove off. Three days and eight hundred miles later we drew up before a building on Viale Umbria in Milan. I followed Avram inside and we went up to the second floor. A door opened and Avram announced: "I have brought Arthur."

"Commander, *shalom,*" I said.

Yehuda Arazi was in his forties, in the prime of life. To the young fellows in their twenties who worked with him in Italy he was "the Old Man." Yehuda was slightly above medium height, but his robust frame and broad shoulders made him appear much taller. His Roman nose, large and penetrating eyes, thick brows and shock of black hair graying at the temples lent him an impressive, almost magnetic, appearance. He had attracted some of the finest men in the Jewish units of the British Army and the Jewish Brigade as well as some skilled Palyam seamen and radio operators.

One of Yehuda's colleagues was Ada Sereni. She had come to Italy after the war to look for her husband, Enzo. (Enzo Sereni's fate, after he parachuted into enemy territory in northern Italy and was captured by the Gestapo, was not immediately known. Only later was it learned that he had perished in an extermination camp.) Ada was a native Italian. Petite, bright, very charming, she was steeped in Italy's culture and enjoyed amazing personal contacts with the higher echelons of Italian society and government. She was the "Foreign Minister" in Yehuda's small "Cabinet," and she did her work with marvelous diligence, charm and ability.

I spent my first evening in Milan reciting our adventures on land and sea. The sea saga was already known in Italy to some extent. Word had come from home that Yaacov, captain of the *Ada,* had kept his word and had notified home headquarters about us as soon as he reached Silipca. From that point, nothing was known about us back home until Yehuda wired that "Arthur and his companions were caught in a Gallipoli brothel . . . "

Ada was now assigned the task of liberating the Italians and the Turks from the Gallipoli jail. This involved political string-pulling. She went to Rome and got in touch with her friends in Naval Intelligence there. She told them about the mishap in Gallipoli and asked for their help. The NI men furnished her with high-level contacts in Lecce, the county seat, and in Gallipoli itself, where the chief of police received direct orders to help her. In two weeks Ada achieved an enviable status in Gallipoli. The mayor and police chief understood that they were dealing with highly-placed friends of the Italian authorities, and that they were to release the prisoners and close the files. The Turks, released first, received their money—not in gold coins, true, but in equally desirable dollars. We felt sure that never again, in any circumstances and for any amount, would they leave Turkish waters.

The Italian sailors went home, and some of them eventually went back to blockade-running.

And Lucia?

A month after leaving Gallipoli I was back, driving an army jeep and wearing an American Army uniform. In my pocket was an officer's ID attaching me to a unit which existed only in the resourceful imagination of our Staff Documentary Unit. My mission was to pay Lucia and the fishermen for everything they had done for us.

I parked the jeep near Via Battisti 12. With the release of the prisoners, Lucia's reputation in Gallipoli had sky-rocketed. Everyone now knew that she had harbored "good" foreigners, on whom shone the benign favor of the regime in Rome.

I knocked on the door. Lucia opened it, drew back a step, then embraced me with a resounding kiss on the lips.

"Why did you do all that for us, Lucia?"

We were sitting in her room, the one with the oversize bed. Before replying, she wanted to know whether I'd be staying overnight. "Yes," I said. She put together a quick meal—spaghetti, cheese, a jug of wine. Then she answered my question.

She was very young, she said, almost a child, when she was married. Her husband was a fisherman. They were together only a few months when, far away in Ethiopia, fighting broke out between Italian troops and the Emperor's forces. The young husband was conscripted. A year later he returned in a hospital ship, wounded in the lungs. She was at his side for months, following him from hospital to hospital. Her daughter was born. The soldier was finally released, given a miserly discharge grant, and sent back to Gallipoli, chronically ill, his lungs all but useless. He was unable to work, and took to drink. Hunger stalked the household. Her sick husband began to beat her mercilessly. To feed the family, Lucia turned to prostitution. Her husband died on the eve of the World War.

"You want to know why I hid you? Believe me, I can tell the difference between criminals, thieves, deserters, and refugees fleeing the police. You didn't look like criminals to me. You were innocent and helpless. That's why I helped you."

"Fine, Lucia. We can never repay you for your good heart, but you must have also spent quite a bit on us. How much was it?"

Lucia went to a chest in the corner of the room and came back with several slips and notes. These were the daily accounts she kept of what she had spent on food, laundry, cigarettes and other items.

She wrote down a figure and handed it to me. I glanced at the slip of paper.

"Come, Lucia, this can't be all. How about the expenses of the fishermen?"

Together we added a sum to cover the loss of a night's fishing. Even so, the total wasn't large at all.

"No other expenses, Lucia?"

She shook her head, but then a thought came to me.

"Lucia, you no doubt lost a few clients while you were looking after us."

She admitted I was right. I felt better. Together with this lost income, the final sum should be respectable. But Lucia protested.

"No, no, don't do that. It isn't necessary."

I insisted. Before we parted, Lucia went back to the chest and took out a photograph of herself.

"What's your name?" she asked.

"Amnon."

She wrote on the back: "Most affectionately to Amnon, from his dear friend Lucia."

I put the photograph in my pocket, got into the jeep, and drove northward.

Savona

MOSSAD'S ITALIAN branch was based in Milan, a convenient area for us. It was the terminus of all the refugee escape channels across Italian-Austrian-Yugoslav borders. Here were organized the "Preparatory Groups," a sort of interim stage before the "Embarkation Camps." Yehuda and his men were in charge of the "Embarkation Camps," which they handled with military precision.

We had four centers in Milan. The small staff was located on Viale Umbria; here were the quarters and workrooms of the branch leaders and veterans. At Magenta we had a farmhouse, which served as our general base. Here we put up the Palyam seamen, the drivers from the Jewish Brigade and other units who had joined us as well as selected immigrants who were eager to help us. Magenta was also where we stored foodstuffs, fuel, ship's gear, and some weapons.

Our third center was a Milan garage, where we kept trucks, jeeps and other vehicles which came to us by devious ways from British and American army units. These vehicles underwent considerable changes in color, serial numbers and papers. The garage housed a group of drivers, alumni of Jewish transport units in the British Army. The fourth and most secret center was a small farm about twenty kilometers from Milan. Here we operated our clandestine radio transmitter, the nerve center of a network which spread all over Italy and kept us in touch with the other branches and with Eretz-Yisrael.

Shortly after I joined Yehuda's staff, we began preparing for an entirely new operation. Until then, most of the blockade-running vessels which sailed from Italy were bought in the local market and were very small vessels. We now received word from headquarters that the Mossad people in the U.S. had acquired two corvettes from U.S. Navy surplus and had sent them to Europe under South American flags. They were now on their way to the Mediterranean, one for our branch in France and one for us. Our corvette would be the largest and soundest vessel we ever had—about eight hundred tons—and could carry about 1,300 refugees. Yehuda immediately put the branch into high gear. We split into three units. One, headed by one of our best veteran seamen, Berchik, was to go down to the port of Savona and get the ship ready. A second, headed by Leska, would transport about a thousand people by truck from the Tardatta camp to the point of embarkation. The third unit, headed by David Solomon and me, would bring four hundred more from Turin to the rendezvous point.

A few days before sailing we decided on the exact point of embarkation, a small fishing jetty at Vado several miles west of Savona itself. Yehuda's orders were for the corvette to approach the darkened jetty about thirty minutes after midnight. Our seamen would bring her as close to the jetty as possible with the aid of pre-arranged signal lights. At 1 A.M. the vessel would be ready to take on the large contingent of a thousand refugees from Tardatta. The second contingent, from Turin, would get there at 1:45, by which time the first group would be aboard. Our four hundred would then follow.

We decided to transport the refugees to Savona in civilian vehicles. We had military trucks but preferred not to use them. "Military" convoys packed with refugees had been caught several months earlier on the La Spezia highway. But how were we to get our hands on civilian vehicles in a period of austerity? Moreover, gasoline and spare parts were obtainable only on the black market.

Ada's friends in Milan put us in touch with a group of former partisans who had made guerrilla incursions against the Germans in northern Italy during the war and were now in possession of thirty-ton Fiats. The drivers of this heavy equipment, who looked like a crew of land pirates, operated these vehicles on all kinds of strange missions. They traveled long distances, from Milan and Turin in the north to Bari and Taranto in the south. Their relations with the police were unique: "You scratch my back, I'll scratch yours."

The driver's cab contained a special cot behind the seat for the driver and his helper to rest on alternately during the long trips. Quite often a female hitchhiker climbed aboard and eased the rigors of travel for young drivers.

David and I were given six large Fiat trucks, each of which was equipped with six rough boards, seating a total of sixty. To be on the safe side, we spread tarpaulins over the truck bodies. A supply of water was placed aboard each truck. We met with the stocky mustachioed drivers and planned our route on a map. We would leave Milan at noon and get to the refugee center in Turin at six in the evening. As we were unfamiliar with the road from Turin to Savona, we had to trust to their judgment. The road, they said, wound through mountains, and the trip south from Turin to the village of Bara, thence across the Tanaro River to Ceba and on to Savona and Vado would take five hours. If we left Turin at seven and allowed an hour and a half for unforeseen developments, we could reach the ship at the scheduled time.

We drove from Milan to Turin, and our Fiats pulled up in the yard of an abandoned barracks on the outskirts of the city where our four hundred refugees were quartered. I knew the man in charge, having met him at our headquarters in Milan. A former partisan, he had been an active Zionist since early youth. We accompanied him to a large hall where our people were gathered. Most were men, but there were also almost a hundred young women. We briefed them on our plan and they listened tensely and quietly. We asked their leader whether there was any serious illness, but they had all been examined by a physician and pronounced fit.

One of the standard instructions given to us was to refuse to accept pregnant women. We knew from experience that they could involve us in difficulties endangering the entire undertaking. However, this instruction was difficult to follow. The life instinct of these young couples married just after the European holocaust was stronger than any directive. Along the escape route, in the "Preparatory Groups" and "Embarkation Camps," the pulse of life among the young people kept up its fertile beat.

"Any pregnant women here?" I asked the leader.

A mischievous twinkle came into his eyes. "I think not."

I turned to the women themselves and repeated the question. To me they all looked suspiciously roundish, especially as they were wearing all the clothes they could, but they smiled and shook their heads.

"O.K.," I said to David. "Let's assume there are no pregnancies here." In a whisper I added, "If you ask me, they all look slightly pregnant."

We divided the people into groups of sixty, and they quickly boarded our Fiats, which we covered with the tarpaulins. We were ready to move. David took his seat in the cabin of the lead truck and I climbed into the rear truck.

Our convoy started out, maintaining a distance of about a hundred yards between trucks. The first hour passed without incident. The night was dark. The road was almost deserted. About eight o'clock in the evening, the third truck pulled up with brakes grinding—a flat in a front tire. We were already in the mountains. The passengers were ordered out, "men to the right, women to the left." The time needed for changing the tire was used to good advantage in communion with nature.

The drivers accomplished the job with dispatch and we were soon on our way again. About ten o'clock, Fiat No. 5 pulled up lame—this time it was a rear tire. The convoy again ground to a halt. The drivers cursed Italian manufacturers and the black marketeers for supplying such shoddy merchandise. By the time the flat tire was repaired, we had lost all the time we had allowed for emergencies. One more flat and we were bound to be late. The road wound among the mountains. Another hour passed without mishap. "In a few minutes we'll reach the bridge across the Tanaro," said the driver to me. "From there on, the road's better."

I could see the bridge clearly in the moonlight. The first truck reached it and stopped, as did the second and the third. The entire convoy stood still. I jumped out and ran forward. David and a few drivers were standing by the bridge. They looked worried, almost panic-stricken. "Look at the bridge," said David. "We're in trouble."

I looked. This was a Bailey bridge which had probably been thrown across the stream by the British Army in place of an original bridge blown up during the war.

David pointed to the tall iron sides. "Arthur," he said, "the Fiats can't make it. They're wider than the bridge."

He was right. The first Fiat had its hood on the bridge but its sides extended beyond the girders on either side, by about two inches.

"Perhaps the other trucks are narrow enough to cross," I suggested.

The drivers shook their heads, but were willing to give it a try. The passengers of trucks Three and Four got off, and their drivers tried to force their way through. Wood grated against metal. Nothing doing. All the Fiats were the same width.

I looked at my watch. We were fifteen minutes behind schedule.

"Now what?" David wanted to know.

The head driver told us that his men had not traveled this road since the war. They knew that the British had put up a new bridge, but they had no idea that it was so narrow. He huddled with the other drivers and finally told us that we could reach Savona by another route, but would have to backtrack about fifteen miles and follow another road for about thirty more miles to a usable bridge.

"That's forty-five miles," I remarked to David. "At least two more hours of travel. We'll be late by about two and a half hours. They won't wait for us, and the ship will leave without our people."

I felt a cold sweat breaking out on my forehead. My throat was constricted. In David's eyes I saw shock. "We have no choice," he groaned. "We must keep on going."

The refugees stood off to one side, tense and anxious. They knew something had gone wrong, but had full confidence in us. We told the drivers to take the alternate route. The refugees were told to climb back into the trucks.

A devastating thought struck me. "What about the other bridge?" I asked the drivers. "Suppose it's blown up? Or what if it turns out to be another Bailey bridge?"

They shrugged. The trucks rolled on.

Luck was with us. The other bridge was undamaged, and the Fiats went across with no trouble. Fifteen more miles and we would be in Savona. The drivers kept the accelerators down to the floor-board. Still, we needed a miracle. If we found the Vado jetty deserted, how would we face our passengers?

At three o'clock in the morning we saw the light of Savona. Half an hour later we were rolling through its empty streets. A few minutes farther on lay Vado.

Suddenly I saw lights on the road—white, red, green. My apprehension was still mounting when the convoy stopped, brakes shrieking. Seconds later we found ourselves surrounded by *carabinieri* and police. Searchlights mounted on jeeps and flashlights in the hands of the policemen bathed our convoy with light. We were ordered out of the trucks.

Leska's voice came from behind the police cordon. "David! Arthur! Take your people with you. Obey the police. They will take you to us. All of us were caught."

I breathed more easily; at least the fate of the Turin group would be no worse than that of the others. We mingled with the hundreds of people from the first convoy. There were now a thousand of us, surrounded by the police cordon. I saw the boat, tied to the jetty, with another line of policemen separating us from the vessel.

Leska gave us a quick report on what had happened. The corvette had arrived at the scheduled time and place. Waiting for it at the jetty were Yehuda, Ada, and a well-known American Jewish journalist, I.F. Stone, who wanted to ride a blockade-runner on its voyage to Palestine. The captain of the corvette, however, had chosen this time to become dead drunk and was in no shape to guide the boat to the jetty. The light signals of our people on shore made no impression on him. The ship zigzagged crazily without reaching the anchorage. The first mate, who was sober enough, tried to take the helm, but the captain, cursing and screaming, repulsed him. Meanwhile, some fishermen sailing back to Vado noticed the erratic maneuvering of the craft in its attempt to come close to the jetty. Thinking that the boat had smugglers aboard, or perhaps even escaped Nazis or Fascists, they alerted the Vado police, who signaled to Savona for reinforcements. Our seamen succeeded in mooring the corvette just as the large convoy arrived from Tardatta with its thousand refugees. But the police also arrived at the same time. Ship and refugees were placed under armed guard.

Ada, Yehuda and Stone entered into immediate and emotional negotiations with the police commanders. Yehuda introduced himself as Dr. Bergman, the representative of the refugees. But it wasn't easy. The Italians were aware at once that they were involved with illegal Jewish immigration, and every police officer in Italy knew very well this was a matter in which one could get his fingers burned. The Savona police had no wish to court trouble. They got in touch with their superiors, threw the hot potato into their laps, and awaited instructions.

Ada, Yehuda and Stone were taken to the police commandant in Savona. Before thy left, Ada begged the commander of the *carabineri* to allow the women to board the vessel.

"Look at them," she appealed. "Each and every one a survivor of the war. Many are pregnant. They traveled in trucks for hours. Would you let them shiver on the pier in this cold?"

The officer nodded and ordered his men to allow the women to go aboard and rest.

"That's where it stands now," concluded Leska. "Yehuda is still in Savona. Berchik and his seamen are aboard with the women."

"We also have women," I said. "They should be allowed to join the others."

We approached the officer in charge. The police wouldn't discriminate against the women from Turin, would they? Permission was granted.

We held a consultation, and a spokesman approached the officer.

"Sir, would you have any objection if the youngsters in the group went aboard? They've been on their feet for hours."

He gazed at us kindly and somewhat sadly. "Go ahead, get the young ones aboard." The men who climbed into the ship might not have qualified for the category in other circumstances, but at four in the morning who was to make the distinction? There were now more people aboard than on the pier. More time went by, and we tried the same tack again.

"Sir, there are the aged and the infirm. Can't they go aboard?"

"Let the elderly go up," the officer instructed the *carabinieri* at the bottom of the gangway.

We now let Leska carry the ball.

"Sir, among the men on the pier are the husbands of the women. I appeal to you not to break up families."

"I will not break up families," agreed the officer tonelessly. He had apparently resigned himself to the inevitable.

All of us were now aboard. The pier was bare, except for the security forces. The people had set themselves up in the hold, ready to sail. But could we? We had to wait for Yehuda.

From the road to the east came a reddish beam of light. A police jeep swept up to the pier and stopped at the gangway. The *carabinieri* sergeant at the wheel waited for Yehuda to get down, then spoke to the officer. The latter nodded, and Yehuda leaped up the gangway. He wanted to know two things: how we had managed to get the people aboard, and whether the convoy had come from Turin. The second question was answered as soon as he saw me in the group, and Leska told him the rest.

Yehuda told us what had taken place in Savona:

The District Governor was waiting for them at police headquarters. When Stone presented his documents and credentials as an "American correspondent accredited by the U.S. Government," the Italians became greatly agitated. As for Ada's presence, not only were the Governor and the Police Commandant impressed by the well-known Sereni name, but they were further confounded by Ada's warning that a refusal to allow the boat to depart might have grave international complications. The Commandant was very unhappy. "Signora," he entreated Ada, "the coast of Italy is very long, it has hundreds of harbors and piers. Why did you have to choose little Vado for your departure point?"

But the Governor conceived a brilliant idea. He put through a call to British intelligence headquarters in Genoa, gave an account of what was going on, and asked for advice. The officer in Genoa promised to call back shortly. Yehuda saw that things were becoming critical, and decided that he had to get back to the ship at all costs. He talked to Stone, who, being hard of hearing, had to use a hearing-aid. The newspaperman now pretended to be extremely put out.

"Gentlemen," he said to the Italians, "you have detained me here for over an hour. The batteries in my hearing-aid are running down. I can hardly hear what you are saying. I have reserve batteries aboard the ship, and I demand that you get them to me."

Yehuda volunteered to go, under armed guard, and bring the batteries. A jeep was placed at his disposal for the purpose—and here they were.

By this time Yehuda had a plan ready.

To me: "Arthur, take Stone's two suitcases to the jeep and act as my porter. When we get to Savona, manage to slip away. Catch the first train to Milan and let them know back home what's happening."

To Berchik: "Get axes. Fifteen minutes after we leave in the jeep, cut the mooring ropes and sail at full speed out to sea. I don't think the *carabinieri* will fire at you. David and the others who aren't sailing are to lower a lifeboat near La Spezia, go to Portovenere and from there to Milan."

Yehuda shook hands with Berchik. I pulled down the visor of my cap, picked up the two suitcases and followed Yehuda to the jeep. The sergeant started the motor. I sat in the rear seat and, as befitted a porter, didn't open my mouth all the way to Savona.

The yard of the Savona police station was a beehive, with policemen, police cars and motorcycles coming and going. Yehuda went upstairs, I and the valises behind him. In the Commandant's office, Yehuda imperiously ordered me to deposit the bags next to Stone's chair and waved me out of the room in the manner of a general dismissing his armor-bearer. All this was done with such ease and self-assurance that no one thought of questioning my coming or going.

I ambled down the stairs and out of the station yard. No one tried to stop me. I caught the first train, bought a newspaper and hid behind it. At ten I was at our Milan headquarters. I shaved, had a quick breakfast, drove to our radio station and reported to home headquarters.

Back in Milan, I found myself almost alone. I waited impatiently for news. Later that evening I learned what had happened in Savona.

The telephone in the Commandant's office rang a few minutes after I left. The Commandant picked up the receiver, listened, grew pale and exclaimed: "She escaped!"

"Who? What?" demanded the Governor.

"The ship! That damned ship!"

"Impossible!" cried Yehuda. "I was just there!"

"Impossible, not impossible!" wailed the Commandant. "That was the commanding officer of the *carabinieri.* They cut the ropes and made off! What shall I do now? What shall we tell the British? They are coming from Genoa."

Weakening batteries or not, Stone was not to be outdone:

"What the hell do I care about the British? I'm an American. My companions and I were to have been aboard that ship on an important assignment, and you let her go! You are to blame for everything! Why did you detain us? Why in the devil's name did you bring us here? I demand that you give me a motorboat. I'll catch up with that damned ship!"

"My dear sir," said the Commandant, much put out. "I didn't bring you to Vado and I haven't detained you. You came of your own free will. If you want to catch up with the ship, go ahead!"

Stone rose angrily, grabbed the valises and marched out of the room, with Ada and Yehuda right behind him. They could almost hear the Commandant's sigh of relief. As they left the building, several British staff cars flashed by them into the yard and pulled up with screeching tires.

The three of them reached Milan early in the afternoon, overcome with fatigue. Leska and other Mossad men arrived about midnight. The corvette had dropped them off exactly where Yehuda had said, at Portovenere near La Spezia. They left the boat with a friend in a shipyard, hired a car and drove to Milan.

The corvette came to a glorious ending. When caught by the British off the shores of the Promised Land, she was bearing a distinguished name and was now the *Josiah Wedgwood,* in honor of one of the most devoted friends the Jewish people had ever had in the British Parliament. When the War of Independence broke out, the *Josiah*

Wedgwood was moored in Haifa harbor along with other battered blockade-runners. Palyam seamen put her in shape and took her to Caesarea, where she was re-outfitted and equipped with cannon and other fighting gear. She then became the *K*-18, a corvette of the Israel Navy.

Portovenere

AFTER THE blockade-runner *Josiah Wedgwood* was forcibly wrested from the Italian *carabinieri* in Vado, barely evading the British, the area became too hot for us. We realized that once again we would have to find new embarkation points on the Italian coast.

Yehuda turned his attention again to the region of the port of La Spezia on the Ligurian Sea. This was characteristic of his daring. Only a few months earlier two of our ships, the *Fede* and *Phoenicia,* had been caught, crowded to the gunwales with refugees. Several of our own men, who had brought the convoys of trucks to the port, were caught (dressed in British uniforms to boot) by the British security forces. The refugees declared a hunger strike, and an international storm developed over the two vessels. Harold Laski, a prominent member of the British Labor Party, visited the ships and subsequently tried to get Foreign Secretary Ernest Bevin to intervene, but with no success. The President of the United States sent a telegram to the head of the British Government. Following these strenuous efforts, the two ships were eventually given a "one-time" and "final" permit to sail for the Promised Land.

In the wake of this episode, the British stationed a special officer at La Spezia to keep constant watch on the port and its immediate vicinity, lest Jews again attempt to use the town as a staging area for "illegal" immigration.

The officer, Major Gordon-Lett, was a beefy, ruddy-cheeked Englishman, with a walrus mustache adorning his round face and thick lips. He had a rich military background and loved the good life: drinking, fishing, and, it goes without saying, young Italian women. He established himself in a very strategic location. He rented a beautiful villa in the picturesque village of Portovenere, which nestled at the tip of a small peninsula extending from La Spezia, like a finger pointing far out into the sea. It was an excellent vantage point, and from it he made many forays in search of Jews, camps, suspicious vehicles and similar quarry. When other officers asked him about his job, his walrus mustache twitched with a grin:

"Jews are my meat," he boasted.

There was a shipyard in the village whose Italian owner was ready to help us. Yehuda, having consulted with Ada and our staff, planned to outfit several ships which would take on passengers from a refugee camp to be set up at the estuary of the Magre River, about fifteen miles south of La Spezia near Carrara, home of the famed marble.

This plan, a very invasion of the lion's den, had a logic all its own. The excitement caused in the area by our activities had brought us a host of Italian friends. Some of them were emotionally affected by our struggle, and others were acquired for cash on the line. We now turned to these friends for help. Our goal was to launch four or five ships in succession, and to make this operation our top priority for the summer of 1946.

Before embarking on this major undertaking, we planned to send one ship out from a point elsewhere on the Italian coast, partly to divert the attention of the British from the La Spezia area. The choice fell on Baccoli, just north of Naples. Like Portovenere, this was also a fishing village located at the tip of a peninsula. A spacious two-story house in Baccoli was the training site for one of our immigrant assembly centers, which were scattered throughout Italy. To this village we now sent Moshe Rabinowitz, an experienced veteran and one of our best Palyam seamen, who had been involved in previous campaigns in La Spezia and had displayed superior qualities of leadership.

Moshe was put in charge of organizing Baccoli for the embarkation. A small vessel, later the *Amiram,* was to arrive in Baccoli directly from France. The operation was synchronized with Shaul in Paris and with our branch in Marseilles. After a few days in Baccoli, Moshe got in touch with us in Milan and reported that he lacked a most important item: two or three craft to transport several dozen people simultaneously from shore to ship.

We checked our inventory to see what we could send. We remembered that in Magenta, a village near Milan, we had a twenty-five-foot German landing-craft intended for crossing rivers or for marine commando operations—an odd craft of light metal, painted green, with a shallow bottom, which our men had "picked up" while they were still in British uniform.

There was also, in the shipyard of our friend in Portovenere, a motor-powered lifeboat which some of our men had used to leave the *Wedgwood* and escape from the Italian and British security forces. Our plan was to have the motorboat tow the landing-craft, and Moshe could thus transfer his passengers from shore to ship.

Our immediate problem was how to haul these cumbersome craft a distance of more than six hundred miles. Yehuda tossed into my lap the responsibility for getting the two vessels to Baccoli quickly. I consulted our drivers, veterans of the British Transportation Corps who had remained in Italy to help Mossad. Together we looked for a vehicle large enough to carry both boats. After a lengthy search, we found a huge Alfa-Romeo truck and trailer. We thought the motorboat would fit into the truck and the landing-craft into the trailer.

Roberto, the driver of the Alfa-Romeo, was short and gaunt, so small that he practically disappeared behind the truck's huge wheel, but he handled his giant vehicle like an expert animal trainer. He knew all the highways and byways—and that meant a great deal to us. He was on friendly terms with the police, the customs people and the innkeepers along all the roads. We planned to use the dirt roads and less well-traveled highways, where traffic would be light during the day, and make up for lost time at night by driving on the main arteries.

That night our people in Magenta loaded the landing-craft into the trailer, where they wrapped it in tarpaulins until it looked like a giant mummy. Roberto and I left at dawn, reached La Spezia by nightfall and continued to Portovenere. There the shipyard crew helped us load the motorboat into the truck, and again we added tarpaulins and miles of rope. Now our rig looked like a monstrous two-hump camel.

For the next two days we drove south. Roberto knew which of the roadside inns served the best food. Our men had long since learned that the best places to eat were those patronized by truck drivers. That's where one got the finest spaghetti, the *zuppa pavese* and the *coteletto Milanese,* even if the kitchen might not have passed sanitary inspection.

Roberto knew exactly how to explain our cargo to the curious truckers with whom we ate. Until we got to Rome, his version was that he was transporting heavy turbines for irrigation projects in the south. I, he proclaimed proudly, was "an expert engineer for pump installations." Then he tired of this tale and switched to another fantasy. The cargo now consisted of silo sections intended for wheat-farming experimental stations. I, the *straniaro,* was an expert at putting the sections together.

We reached the outskirts of Naples. To get to Baccoli we had to go through the metropolitan area, which was crawling with British soldiers and sailors. We rolled into the city toward nightfall. The Alfa-Romeo, rumbling heavily along the narrow streets, could not help but attract attention.

I kept a tense lookout in the side mirror. We were almost out of Naples when the mirror showed a military jeep following us. I said to Roberto: "Slow down and keep to the right. Let him pass us." The jeep went by, and as it did, the driver leaned far out and took a good look at us.

Once in front of us, the jeep seemed in no hurry. Soon it slowed down, and we had no alternative but to pass it. Then again it passed us and the driver repeated his leapfrogging maneuver. Roberto shared my mounting nervousness as we reached the suburbs.

"I'm putting on more speed," said Roberto. The Alfa-Romeo lurched forward. "A few more miles and we'll be in Pozzuoli. I'll try to get rid of him there."

Near Pozzuoli, a small village midway between Naples and Baccoli, Roberto swung the heavy truck at a sharp angle into a side street. The jeep stayed on the main highway, which made us feel slightly better. We remained on the side street for a few minutes, then took a roundabout way to the highway. Baccoli indeed seemed to be near at hand. But a few hundred yards out of Pozzuoli I looked into the mirror and got a jolt. The jeep was behind us again. He had simply waited for us at the exit from the village.

Roberto stuck his head out of the window and took a long look behind: "The driver is a British soldier, with a red hat."

"That's an M.P.," I groaned. "Looks like we're trapped."

Less than a mile away from Baccoli the jeep flashed by us and screeched to a halt across the narrow road, blocking it completely. We stopped. A British soldier jumped out of the jeep and bounded up to the step of the cab. At first I saw only his red paratroop beret, then I recognized his features.

"Dov!" I yelled. "Dov!"

The "British soldier" was Dov Berger of Kibbutz Bet Oren,

with whom I had served in a British Army artillery unit during the war. I hadn't seen Dov for two years. He had volunteered for the paratroops and was parachuted behind enemy lines in Rumania to gather information, help Jews escape, and do some sabotage. He was eventually captured by the Gestapo. I later heard that he had been released when the war was over, and immediately plunged into rescue work in Rumania. I jumped out of the truck and embraced him.

Dov told me that he had been in Naples for several days, together with several former British prisoners—pilots and paratroopers. The British in Naples were treating them like heroes, giving them vehicles, money and furloughs before sending them home. He had been cruising along in his jeep in the streets of Naples when he saw the Alfa-Romeo and spotted a familiar face next to the driver. "I know that face, but from where?" He decided to investigate. He passed us several times. "That's Lova? Looks like Lova, but—." Finally he had decided to stop us and find out.

I told Dov where I was going, and he begged me to let him help. I joined him in the jeep and we drove to the camp in Baccoli. Moshe, waiting impatiently for his boats, was overjoyed.

A few nights later, little *Amiram* sailed from Baccoli for the Promised Land.

We were now ready for the operation in the north, in the La Spezia area. An advance unit reached Bocca del Magre and began setting up a base at the estuary. The shipyard people stood by to outfit the four vessels which Yehuda had acquired from various sources.

The presence of Major Gordon-Lett was a thorn in our side, and we spent many hours planning how to rid ourselves of this danger. We happened to learn that he was looking for an assistant, a sort of local secretary. He had convinced his superiors that he was working under heavy strain and that he needed a "native" to serve him as eyes and ears.

Ada suggested that we try to fill this post with one of our Italian friends, and we chose a certain Aldo Restani, a writer. Aldo loved us and our work. He was young, almost a boy, of medium height, very slim with handsome features that seemed carved out of marble and a head of unruly jet-black hair. Aldo was a perfect example of the "dolce vita" generation of young Italians then in its infancy—a bittersweet generation, sentimentally cynical, anxious yet carefree. He applied for the job and, with his enchanting smile, was immediately hired.

Aldo lost no time in twisting the Major around his little finger. He fed him stories about "suspicious movements" on our part, which always took place where we were not. He drafted impressive reports. With Aldo's help, Yehuda decided to get the Major away from the area during the crucial month of August.

The scorching July heat around La Spezia simplified Aldo's task of persuading the Major to take a vacation in northern Italy in the refreshing mountain climate, especially as it would cost him nothing. Aldo had relatives at Lake Como, and they would be happy to accommodate the Major. Then, too, there was Aldo's cousin, a beautiful girl. Aldo saw to it that the beautiful "cousin" would be waiting for the Major at Lake Como—one of those ladies in plenty on the beaches of the lake, for a price. Aldo paid her handsomely and coached her carefully in the role she was to play. The Major was due for an interesting month in Como, and so were we—in La Spezia.

We now swung into action. To Bocca del Magre we brought three vessels, and put aboard them hundreds of refugees arriving at the embarkation camp from all over Italy. We acquired the fourth boat, later to be known as *Four Freedoms*. This vessel, like the others, was to reach the estuary at night.

We chartered three motor-powered fishing boats, manned them with our own crews, and were ready to ferry the refugees in groups of thirty to forty from the river to the ship. Half an hour before embarkation time, all the refugees were at the riverbank near the fishing-boat basin.

Yehuda waited in one of the camp huts until the camp commander reported that all was ready. He emerged from the hut and stood in the area surrounded on three sides by refugees with knapsacks on their backs.

Three deep they stood in long lines, a solid mass of humanity faintly visible in the almost total darkness. The green-and-red lanterns of the fishing boats shed a faint glow. The refugees waited.

"Blockade-runners," began Yehuda, his voice hoarse with fatigue and emotion, "tonight you will be boarding a battleship of the Jewish people. I have been saying these words to every group like yours just before they embarked. This time my words have special meaning. The British are now using new methods. When they captured two of our ships off the coast of Eretz-Yisrael several days ago, they forcibly transferred the refugees to deportation ships and took them to special camps—to concentration camps—in Cyprus."

Yehuda paused for a moment, and I could see that the words "camps, concentration camps" had pierced these young people, all survivors of concentration camps, like daggers.

"We here and your commanders at sea will do everything we can to avoid capture and put you ashore in our homeland safely. However, if the British do catch you, you are to resist them with all your might, to fight off, with your hands and fists, any soldier who attempts to take you off the ship. On the two ships which were captured, the refugees met force with force, and several were injured. You are now soldiers of our people in its fight for survival and for its land. Your predecessors' struggle to reach their homeland was hard, but yours will be much harder. We have no way of knowing how long you will be kept in the camps if you are caught.

"Since neither you nor I knew about the Cyprus camps when you got here, I have decided that you will be given a choice. Anyone who doesn't think he will be able to take the fighting and the beatings, or life in the camps, may now leave the ranks and stay here. You have five minutes to decide."

Silence hung heavy in the air. No one uttered a sound. Yehuda kept glancing at the illuminated dial of his watch.

"All right," he said. "Everybody aboard."

The camp commander, who had been standing off to one side, now assumed command. A few minutes later, the blockade-runner approached the river estuary and signaled that it was ready.

I reached the ship in the first fishing-boat, along with about thirty men. The crew lowered a rope ladder, but the heavy seas made the climb dangerous. The seamen were worried. "How can we get the people aboard tonight? The storm's getting worse, and they're having trouble climbing up."

Up to now, we had been fairly lucky. On embarkation nights the sea had been completely calm, or nearly so. But now the sea began to boil in earnest. The second boat could hardly make fast to the side of the ship and its passengers found it hard to grasp the rope ladders. One ladder tore loose from the boat while two men were climbing it and began swaying like a pendulum.The men clung to it desperately while the seamen pulled them aboard.

The people in the second boat were all finally hauled aboard, and the boat returned to shore. When the third boatload arrived, we were sure it would be impossible to get the people up the rope ladders. The waves were rising higher and higher. We tried a new method. We removed a section of rail aboard the ship and then had the people in the fishing-boat go up on its bridge, which was two yards higher than its deck and roughly level with our own deck. "Jump!"—and the first man in line jumped from their boat to ours. "Jump!"—and another man made the leap. "Jump!" "Jump!" It was especially hard for the women. They landed on our tossing ship like limp sacks of meal, and it was all they could do to stagger away or be helped to the hold. The seamen were no less exhausted than the passengers. The sea grew rougher and rougher. "Jump!" It was now three o'clock in the morning. In another hour day would dawn, and the ship would have to weigh anchor and leave.

"Jump!" The next man in line jumped, but just then the boat swung away from the ship and he fell into the water. A rope ladder was at once lowered and he began climbing out of the seething water. Just as he was abreast of the deck, a wave hurled the boat at him. His cry of pain was drowned in the thunder of the two boats colliding. The seamen managed to pull him aboard.

He was badly hurt. Splinters of bone showed through his legs, which were covered with blood. We knew that he had suffered internal injuries as well, and that he must be taken ashore if he was to live. Two of our men were returning the boat. From the bridge, Yehuda called out to me: "Arthur, the work here will get done without you. Jump into the fishing-boat, take the man ashore and get him to a hospital."

Once on the beach, our medical orderly stopped the flow of blood as best he could. We put the injured man on a stretcher, placed it in our small truck, and made him as comfortable as possible, with his head near the driver's seat.

I drove fast but carefully, knowing that the slightest jolt would add to his suffering. From time to time I took one hand from the wheel and placed it in his. From his lips trickled a thin stream of blood; he had bitten them to keep from crying out. His pallid face was covered with sweat. He was fully conscious. Occasionally a repressed moan escaped his lips. He asked for a cigarette, and I lit one for him, then a second and a third.

We reached the hospital shortly before dawn. The gate-keeper and the orderly on duty helped me get him into the emergency room. Two nuns in white asked me a few routine questions, but not where or how the man had been injured. They knew, as did everyone in town, what was going on on the banks of the river, who the *profugi ebrei* were and where they were going.

I waited outside while a doctor examined the wounded man. After some time he came out and said,

"Both legs are broken. I am calling the surgeon. I think he should undergo surgery as quickly as possible."

I asked him whether it would be necessary to amputate.

"I don't know," he replied. "The surgeon will decide while he's operating."

I went back to the patient. He had been given sedative injections. He grasped my hand tightly.

"I know my condition is bad," he said. "I'm afraid they'll cut off my legs. What will happen to me?"

I tried to console him, but he said:

"You don't understand. Now I won't be able to go on to Eretz-Yisrael."

"We'll worry about that later," I told him.

"Who'll worry?" he exclaimed. "At best, I'll lie many months in a cast and then be a lame cripple. Who'll see to it that I get there?"

"The Old Man will," I replied, "and his men. As soon as you get on your feet, you'll be placed aboard ship. You won't lose your turn."

He gazed at me with his deep, black Jewish eyes.

"Is that true? You will do it?"

"We'll do it," I assured him.

The surgeon arrived and the wounded man was taken to the operating room. I took leave of him with a long handshake.

I never saw him again. But several months later I was sent to work at our main headquarters in Paris. During a phone conversation with our Italian branch, I asked about the patient.

"You know Yehuda," was the reply. "He saw to it that the man got the best care. He sent the best doctors. A week ago, he put him on a boat—cast, crutches and all."

Bogliasco Palace

YEHUDA'S INSTRUCTIONS were these:

Go to Genoa. See our friend Dr. Avigdor. He will help you. Find a suitable embarkation point on the Italian Riviera, between Genoa and La Spezia. We want to house several hundred people and store supplies, ship's gear and weapons.

Dr. Avigdor was an assimilated Jew, a respected shipping agent who was attracted to our work. He knew Genoa like the palm of his hand. His office was in one of the picturesque alleys of Old Genoa —the seaport of Geiona of the Middle Ages. He greeted me in a tastefully appointed room, lavishly decorated with ancient maps and handsomely fashioned brass ship's lanterns.

"My dear Signor Arturo," he said, "what you should do is find and lease one of the old princely or millionaires' palaces—good, solid structures built before the great wars, when the world was still sane. There are quite a few such villas scattered between Genoa and Rapallo, and many have private yacht basins. Let me have a few days, and I shall try to have precise details for you."

I registered in a nearby hotel, posing as a travel agent. Two days later I called Dr. Avigdor.

"Signor Arturo, I think I have just the place. A few miles south of Nervi, right on the water near the small village of Bogliasco, stands the family palace of Prince Adonolfi. The Prince was a wealthy man, a member of Genoa's nobility at the close of the past century. He built the palace near a small cove. The palace, its grounds and the cove are now the property of his aged widow, the Princess Adonolfi. Two of her sons were killed in the war and she is now living in the gatekeeper's lodge. The building needs a good deal of repair work—it served as staff headquarters for the German Navy in Italy during the war. The Princess is quite poor now, and she would like to find a tenant for this giant house, but of course there are no takers for such a magnificent ruin."

We went in Dr. Avigdor's Fiat to see the place. The ten miles from Genoa took us along the beautiful, winding road of the Italian Riviera up to Rapallo.

We passed the picturesque resort town of Nervi and approached Bogliasco, a small village nestling between the slopes of the green hills and the blue sea whose houses were built on both sides of the serpentine road. At the southern edge of Bogliasco, Dr. Avigdor slowed down.

"Here we are," he said.

The palace was surrounded by a high stone fence veiled with creeping vines. The heavy iron gate was elaborately decorated. To the right was a small two-story stone house, the gatekeeper's lodge. Beyond the house was a large garden which had obviously once been well tended. A lane flanked by tall, slim cypresses led to the palace, a massive four-story mansion.

"There is a small but deep inlet behind the house," explained Dr. Avigdor. "The Princess lives here, in the gatekeeper's house."

I returned to Milan. The next day I came back to Genoa in an "American" jeep. (Our garage contained military vehicles of all types and for all purposes.) I wore an American officer's uniform with Joint Distribution Committee insignia. During the war the Joint Distribution Committee had enjoyed quasi-military status, and its men, who came in the wake of the American forces, wore military uniforms. From time to time we assumed their identity.

On this spring day, about noon, I parked my jeep near the gate of the palace in Bogliasco and pulled the bell-rope. A corpulent peasant woman came out of the gatekeeper's house, opened the gate and asked me what I wanted. Well, an American officer wanted to talk to her mistress. Would I wait a while? Of course. The woman returned. The Princess would be glad to see me.

I was led up a flight of stairs to a gloomy chamber. The furniture was old and massive, the remains of palatial glory. A woman rose from an armchair and I bowed as courteously as I could.

Princess Adonolfi was every bit of eighty, tall and thin. Her finely lined face was pale. Her eyes, once doubtless a beautiful blue, were watery. She wore a lace dress and long black scarf. Her bearing seemed to say: *I am of the nobility. Neither my circumstances nor my age can distort the truth.*

In "basic Italian," garnished here and there with high-flown

English, I introduced myself as Captain Keller, an American. I told the Princess that I was looking for a place where the men of my unit, now stationed near Milan, could relax and bathe in the sea. I had heard in Genoa that the Adonolfi palace was one of the finest on the Italian Riviera, and my own view of it certainly substantiated the description.

"My dear Captain," said the Princess, "the house my husband built here was our home for thirty years. We had homes in Rome and Genoa, but this was our favorite. My husband has been dead ten years now, and the palace has been neglected. At first I lived there alone, as my family resides elsewhere. Then came the Germans. They expropriated the house and settled themselves in it. I had to move to Genoa. After the war I found the place in ruins. My limited means allowed me only to repair the gatekeeper's lodge and I live there. If you have the money to refurbish the interior a bit, you will have a beautiful place indeed. The gardens were once glorious, and the inlet is beautiful. This can be just what you want. The renovating will be at your expense, but the rental will not be high."

I asked for permission to see the palace and the grounds. She readily agreed. "I shall send the gatekeeper to accompany you."

The gatekeeper, an easy-going, portly and talkative villager, joined me. We walked up the avenue of cypress and entered the palace. It was built in simple but severe painstaking style, entirely unpretentious, reflecting the character of its aristocratic owner. The ground floor contained several rooms and a glassed-in terrace which overlooked the horseshoe-shaped inlet below. The three upper stories, I found, had many rooms, all of them spacious. In the basement were storerooms and a huge kitchen.

The house was in bad shape. The gatekeeper, too, told me that the palace had served as staff headquarters for special units of the German Navy. When the Nazis left, it was a shambles. They hacked and burned the furniture and stole everything of value. For some time afterwards people were afraid to go into the palace, for the Germans had announced that they had mined the place with time bombs and booby traps. The building could easily accommodate five hundred people and more. I asked the gatekeeper to show me the gardens and inlet.

The extensive gardens had been neglected for a long time. Trees and bushes grew wild. Still, it was possible to walk along red and white gravel paths which led to charming nooks. Here and there were sculptured fountains, long since dry. We descended a steep and narrow staircase to the inlet, a tiny cove whose radius was no more than twenty yards. It was overhung with grayish-white cliffs. At the water's edge was a narrow strip of clean, white gravel. The water in the cove was a deep blue. I asked how deep it was.

"Very deep. One can dive from the cliffs without fear."

The sheltered cove, then, was also satisfactory. I went back to the Princess and said;

"Signora, your house is one of the most beautiful I have ever seen. Of course, it's in awful shape. My unit will have to put a tremendous amount of labor and money into making it habitable. But the place is so wonderful that we're willing to do it. With your permission, we shall rent the house, garden and cove for the summer season."

I suggested that the agreement should also include the house in which she was living. Many soldiers would be coming, "and perhaps some refugees in the care of the American forces." She would be disturbed by the noise and the military movements. On the other hand, she should have no difficulty in finding temporary quarters for herself and the gatekeeper's family in Bogliasco or Nervi, for which we would make additional payment. The Princess accepted my suggestion in good spirit. She specified a very modest sum, and I gave her a handsome deposit. I asked when I could bring the "advance unit." In a week, she said.

I returned to Genoa, where I asked Dr. Avigdor to prepare a lease. Then I went on to Milan, reaching our quarters in Viale Umbria in the evening. I reported to Yehuda, and we decided to have a small unit of "Americans" go to the palace in a few days. Yehuda suggested that I take Zorik and Falik, of the Mossad base in Magenta. We would prepare the palace for the blockade-runners, clean it up, make it habitable and lay in supplies.

Zorik got behind the wheel of our "American" jeep. He was a talented driver with a sixth sense at the wheel but a speed demon, totally oblivious to such things as brakes, foot or emergency. He had been one of the youngest soldiers in the Jewish Brigade, and served briefly with the British Army before volunteering for work with Aliya Bet. Zorik, the son of Dvorah and Shmuel Dayan of Nahalal and the younger brother of Moshe, was an unusual man. Broad-shouldered, with a strong neck, curly hair and mischievous eyes, he behaved in easy and unsophisticated fashion. But within this athletic frame was hidden the soul of a true poet. He wrote verses to his girl friend back home and was most sensitive to beauty and nature. This strange combination made him exceptional even in our unusual outfit.

Falik, the third member of our party, was the youngest Palyam seaman in Italy. He was of medium height, with sparse chestnut hair, and smiling eyes. He was full of quiet energy.

We set out for Genoa, where I had enough money—dollars and lire—to rent and refurbish the palace. We loaded the jeep with field cots, sleeping bags and personal gear. We also took along some signs reading, in English and Italian, *Vacation Camp,* which we were to attach to the palace fence. We had two weeks of hard work ahead of us, and then the first group of immigrants would take up quarters there before embarking for Eretz-Yisrael.

At the palace, we had the Princess sign the proper papers. She was ready to move. The gatekeeper and his family stayed on for a while. In a single day, they helped us recruit scores of workmen from Bogliasco, especially plumbers and electricians, to repair the palace and re-install the water and lighting systems. The big house had an accumulation of dirt, and we had it cleaned and fumigated. The villagers were happy. Italy was undergoing a serious post-war depression. There was no tourism. Most of the British and American troops were gone. Unemployment weighed heavily on the land, especially the Riviera, which was dependent on income from yachtsmen and vacationers. Even our small undertaking was a boon to a small place like Bogliasco. Whenever we went down to the village for a jug of wine, we were welcomed with great rejoicing.

I wrote an impressive letter in English to the Director of Posts in Genoa. I said that we were opening an "American vacation resort" in Bogliasco, and asked that telephone communications be restored to the palace—at our expense, of course—and that a number of telephones be put in so that I might be able to keep in touch with my staff and with various units. The letter did what it was supposed to do; a year's prepayment for service was even more effective. We received "top priority." A few days later we had our telephones.

Gradually we let the gatekeeper and some of the villagers know that we essentially engaged, on behalf of the American forces, in caring for orphans, refugees and displaced persons. Our vacation resort was to make it possible for these survivors of the war to rest, bathe on Bogliasco's wonderful beach, and enjoy life, all at the expense of the Americans.

Falik tested the depth of the water in our private cove. We judged that it was deep enough for vessels up to five hundred tons.

Yehuda telephoned us from Milan. We were to make ready for several hundred people who would be arriving from the Turin area and would stay in the palace a short while before going south to "Siberia," the code name for the large embarkation camp at the mouth of the Magre River. The palace was to serve the immigrants as a way station.

Suddenly, a courier from headquarters came with urgent orders to prepare to deal with an emergency. That very night our people would be bringing a motor convoy from the French Riviera, following a most extraordinary exploit in southern France.

Our procurement people in France had suffered a serious setback. Allied forces discovered and confiscated an arms cache we had assembled—Bren-guns, sub-machineguns and rifles. The arms were left with a French police commandant near Marseilles pending the arrival of the British to collect them. "Simon the Younger"—Yitzhak Levy, a procurement veteran—and a party of his men, all wearing British uniforms, drove to Marseilles in a convoy of "British" trucks. They showed the commandant proper documents instructing him to hand the arms over, which he obediently did. Now our men were driving down to Italy, intending to deliver the arms to us for safekeeping. Zorik and I waited for them in our American jeep at an intersection just north of Genoa.

At eight P.M., exactly as scheduled, a British army jeep rolled up to the intersection. By the light of the street lamps I recognized Simon, in his British uniform with Yohanan at his side behind the wheel. I advanced to be recognized, and Simon said, in English:

"We'll be right back."

The jeep disappeared, but returned a few minutes later, leading a convoy of four covered British trucks. We started out as they approached, and led them through Genoa to Bogliasco. Jeeps and trucks were swallowed up in the darkness of the palace gardens. The men climbed down from their vehicles, exhausted from the long drive. Nevertheless, we set to work at once, and by the time dawn broke the entire cargo was stored in the deep wine-cellar of the palace. The men snatched a hasty snack and drove off to return to France. A few nights later the arms were taken east to one of our main depots in Italy.

Our first batch of immigrants, the Salvino orphans, arrived by night-train, under the care of "Simon the Elder." This "Simon" —Shabtai Luzinsky—was an extraordinary man, a veteran Zionist who had traveled widely for the movement. He was now in his fifties, "too old for anything" by the standards of us youngsters in our twenties. He was one of the first settlers of the village of Atarot in the Jerusalem hills. The years of hard work in the stony hills had left their mark. He was as thin as a rail, but muscular, and his lined face told its tale of toil and sweat, in the sun and wind.

Immediately following the war we had been visited by quite a number of emissaries, whom we somewhat deprecatingly referred to as "Zionists." These were generally members of settlements of various ideologies. They organized and trained the Jewish refugees before turning them over to the Mossad for the final dash to Eretz-Yisrael. They played an important role. We did not have the man-power to handle the thousands of Jews before their arrival at the embarkation points. At the same time, there was a certain amount of perhaps natural antagonism between the "civilian" emissaries from home and ourselves, the veteran members of the underground, organizers of the embarkation camps, procurers and outfitters of ships, captains, seamen and wireless operators. We were extremely careful not to admit them either to our premises or secret plans.

But there were exceptions, and the most exceptional was "Simon the Elder." He couldn't be taken lightly. Even we, the young ones, the cynics and the deprecators, were compelled to respect this man. He was obviously burning himself out in his tireless work for the refugees. He was completely immersed in it, day and night. He did not differentiate between menial and important tasks. Anything that could help our progress toward our goal—rescuing Jews and bring-ing them to the land of their fathers—was of equal importance to him. He was prepared to shine the shoes of our men who were han-dling *aliya*—and I suspect that secretly he did. He was ready to accept any authority and obey any orders that would advance the cause. He sought no honor—only that he be allowed to work and help.

The Salvino children had a special place in our hearts. Salvino was an institution created lovingly by the men in the Jewish units of the British army at the end of the war, for the purpose of caring for numerous orphans hovering around camps and convoys, orphaned boys and girls with frightened eyes and horrible memories. These waifs had been gathered up by young teachers in these units, men like Moshe Ze'iri and his friends. Unit commanders closed their eyes to the disappearance of food and supplies from company stores, and the men were able to clothe, feed and educate the children in Salvino, a beautiful village by whose name the project came to be known.

"Simon the Elder" was now in charge of about a hundred boys and girls between thirteen and seventeen who had been at Salvino for over a year. Simon considered them ready for transfer to the Promised Land, and he left no stone unturned to have them put on the immigration schedule.

The days that these youngsters spent at the palace were lively ones. We could not permit them to venture beyond the outer gate, but within the palace ground they were as free as birds. They could also swim in the cove, under adult supervision. The kitchen functioned efficiently. Food was plentiful.

"Simon the Elder," the veteran farmer, was the first to rise in the morning, and was already busy at dawn. He helped light the ovens in the kitchen for breakfast. He visited "his" children's sleeping quarters to see that they were all right. During the day he never left them. They loved him almost instinctively, almost as if he was their father. He formed a link between the children and us—the somewhat tough and practical soldiers. They felt that as long as "Simon the Elder" was with them they would come to no harm.

From our forward headquarters in Camp "Siberia" to the south came orders to send the Salvino children there by night-train. This was to be their last night in Bogliasco. After a light supper, the boys lined up for inspection. One of them suddenly began to cough violently and seemed to be having trouble breathing. Simon had him lie down, but the coughing grew worse. The boy's face was turning white, then purple, in his efforts to suppress the coughing. At last he gave way. Blood burst from his nostrils and mouth and streamed over his neck and shirt. The boy relaxed somewhat and lay motionless.

"Tuberculosis," Simon said apologetically. He knew we would be angry. The sick were expressly barred. "A doctor who examined him in Salvino said that if he reached Eretz-Yisrael within a month or two, he might not have an attack until then. I took a chance. I hope you forgive me."

The boy, realizing that there was no hope now of his continuing with his friends, covered his chalk-white face with his hands and began to sob quietly but violently.

"I cannot go with the convoy," Simon said. "I would like to have one of you go along with the youngsters to 'Siberia.' I would have to bid them farewell there, anyway—now I'll say good-bye to them here instead. I'll stay with the boy tonight."

The convoy left. I went to the village and brought a doctor to the palace. He examined the boy, gave him a few sedatives and left. Simon sat with the young patient for hours, comforting him until he fell asleep. Then he brought in a cot, set it alongside the boy's bed and lay down fully clothed, his hand—gnarled, calloused, kindly—holding the boy's hand.

The next day "Simon the Elder" took the boy north. Two months later Simon was killed in a road accident while on his way to one of the camps.

The Milan-Paris Express

MORE AND more ships were running the blockade. New Mossad branches were being established throughout Europe. Shaul transferred his headquarters from Tel Aviv to Paris. Yehuda's Italian branch, which had been serving as a sort of school for blockade-running organizers and ship supervisors, was now asked to send some of its people to other places. Shaul summoned me to Paris.

According to the papers I carried I was Sergeant Richard Smith of the Third Tank Battalion of the Royal Tank Corps, stationed in Trieste. I had been granted a special furlough by my Battalion Commander to visit my aged mother in Paris. I was, for all purposes that mattered, a British sergeant: the black beret of the Armored Corps, polished boots, the African Front ribbon with the Eighth Army emblem, and the Italian Front ribbon. Only two years earlier I had indeed been a sergeant in a Jewish unit of the British Army, and I wore the guise easily. My credentials were flawless and inspired me with the proper confidence. The work was Reuven's. Among other things, he was in charge of our camouflage. His impeccably arranged storehouse contained uniforms, printed forms, seals and special equipment from all the armies which flooded Italy after the war.

It was noon. The Milan railway station was thronged with people, including many Allied soldiers—British, American, French. From a distance I saw pairs of British Military Police patrolling the platforms. I hastened to move out of their visual range. When the train was about to leave I elbowed my way through the crowd and clambered aboard one of the packed cars. The train moved out of the yard and started for points north.

A journey from Italy to France, in those days, was quite an operation. Trains were few and far between. The Italian govenment did not yet have full control. Troop movements were still interfering with regular civilian transportation. Passports for civilians involved complicated procedures. The over-age cars were jammed to capacity; people, valises, bundles without end. I was luckily able to wedge myself into a bit of space in the corridor. It did not even enter my mind to try to find a seat in a compartment. I lowered my knapsack to the floor between my ankles and reconciled myself to the prospect of a day or so on my feet or, at best, squatting on the knapsack. I stood there by the window, watching the spires of the Milan Cathedral fade in the distance. Suddenly I heard a feminine voice.

"Sergeant, won't you come into our compartment?"

I turned around. A young woman, black of eye and hair, was leaning out of a compartment and smiling at me.

"Beg your pardon, Miss—you mean me?"

"Yes, Sergeant, you. Why stand in the corridor? Join us in our compartment."

I hesitated. I didn't want to exploit my British identity any more than I had to. True, I had ample command of the language, but why run risks? Still, the English spoken by the young lady had a definite Italian accent. Who else was in the compartment? Perhaps British or American servicemen. But how could I graciously refuse?

"Thanks, Miss. You're sure I won't be intruding?"

"Intruding? No, no! On the contrary, the other girls and I would love to entertain a British sergeant, really."

"Other girls." I breathed a little more easily. I picked up my knapsack and went inside. I found smiling, colorfully dressed Italian girls, four in all, sitting amid a vast array of valises, baskets and bundles. "Allow me to introduce ourselves. I am Maria, this is another Maria, and these are Rosita, and Margaretta. We're delighted."

"My name's Richard. Delighted to meet all of you."

They made room for me between one of the Marias and Margaretta. I stowed my knapsack on their bundles. Maria, the one who invited me in, spoke better English than the others, although it was far from perfect. She lost no time telling me that all four of them were Neapolitans who had married English soldiers about a year earlier. Their husbands were now out of the service and had sent them passports, and they were on their way to Great Britain.

I was very glad for them, and told them so.

"Our country will now be richer by four pretty ladies," I assured them.

They broke into tinkling laughter.

"Sergeant, where are you from in England?" asked Maria. "Where were you born?"

"London."

"You must tell us lots and lots about England." They showed me their fresh British passports. Their new names were Mrs. Maria Thompson, Mrs. Rosita MacBride, Mrs. Maria Goldberg, Mrs. Margaretta Jones. Mrs. Thompson and Mrs. Goldberg were going to be Londoners. Mrs. Jones was going to make her home in Herefordshire, while Mrs. MacBride was headed for Inverness in Scotland.

I had never been in England, but this drawback did not worry me. Not for nothing had Mr. Grossman and Mrs. Norman, our teachers at Tel Aviv's Herzliah High School, fed us descriptions of the English countryside, personalities and atmosphere. Not in vain had we memorized large chunks of Wordsworth, Shelley and Keats. Nor was it a waste of time to have struggled over *The Pickwick Papers, David Copperfield, The Forsyte Saga,* and other standard works.

The compartment grew warm. I removed my tunic, rested my head on Maria's shoulder and said:

"Well, my dears, let me tell you all about England and Scotland."

I ranged far and wide—up, down and across the British Isles. I described the beauties of the lake district, the meadows of Gloucester, the picture villages of Herefordshire, Edinburgh Castle and Westminster Abbey, Big Ben and magnificent Windsor Castle.

I asked Mrs. Maria Goldberg about her husband. Yes, he was an *ebreo*. I approved.

"We English don't discriminate against any religion. We are civilized, tolerant. Your mother-in-law will probably be a second mother to you and teach you how to prepare wonderful Jewish dishes . . . " The charming Italian ladies hung on every word.

It was growing dark. The girls took off their dresses and donned robes which revealed more than they concealed. They felt no embarrassment in my presence. It was as though I were a close relative. Before their marriage to the sons of Britain they were probably "dancers" or "entertainers," and felt little compunction about shedding a few garments.

From their bundles now came dry salamis, excellent Italian cheeses, fresh black bread and fat-bellied bottles of *vino rosso*. For my part,

I contributed cans of bullybeef and some bars of army chocolate, a highly valued commodity. We enjoyed a banquet. When it was finally over, Maria produced a mandolin and accompanied herself in a medley of popular Neapolitan ballads, to which her companions added the sweet and sentimental melodies of southern Italy. The singing floated out of the compartment. Passengers repeatedly poked their heads in, only to withdraw hastily with *scusi, scusi!*

At the Swiss border, the train halted for a lengthy and thorough inspection by Italian and Swiss customs officials and constables. By the time they reached our compartment, I had collected the four blue British passports of the *signoras* and placed my own travel papers on top: Sergeant Richard Smith, on his way to Paris to meet his ailing mother, who had made the trip from Dover to see her son. The constables knocked on the door. I gave them the entire packet. They had a hard time keeping their eyes away from the bared arms of the girls. Certainly the documents received far less attention. I offered the constables some English cigarettes, and each of them accepted only one. More might be construed as a bribe. They apparently thought that I was the leader of this "bridal excursion" from Naples to London, and gave my papers a cursory glance. The officials beamed at the young ladies, and I, too, came in for a good deal of respect because I was engaged in the worthy task of reuniting Italian wives with their British husbands.

The next day I was in Paris.

Peruwelz

In Paris I worked for a time with Shaul and his small staff and particularly with Ehud Avriel, and was then assigned to our Belgian branch. I was given quarters in the home of Professor Perlman of the University of Brussels, whose wife, Fella, was active in our refugee and immigration work. My room was on the top floor of their suburban home.

Willy, the head of the branch, described my assignment. Three wooden vessels, purchased by Ehud from a Greek shipdealer, were moored in Swedish ports, without crews. It was difficult, almost impossible, to find Scandinavian seamen for our "shady" operations or "illegal" ships, even at high wages. Our people in Paris therefore believed the ships should be manned by Spanish Republican seamen, unemployed refugees who were haunting Marseilles by the hundreds. These sailors would sail these vessels, under the command of one or two of our seamen, from Sweden to France or Italy, where the ships would be outfitted for the voyage to Eretz-Yisrael. Willy explained why Belgium had been selected as the route from France to Sweden.

"In Antwerp I found a shipping agent who was willing, for a price, to transport Spanish sailors without papers directly to our ships in Sweden. We now have all the necessary connections."

All but one, it seemed. Still missing was the method of smuggling the sailors out of France and into Belgium. This was to be my job.

I approached some professional border smugglers, but they refused. We then decided to seek the help of French Jews near the Belgian border in whose homes we could conceal the Spanish sailors until we could find a way of spiriting them across the line. Once they were inside Belgium, it would be no problem to load them on trucks which could deliver them to Antwerp within three hours.

A brief survey led us to Valenciennes, where several hundred Jewish families had resettled after the war. A Jewish youth group had organized there, with its own club, and about a hundred boys and girls were now studying its various programs—such as Hebrew, Zionism and scouting. The Paris branch helped us make contact with Jacques, the group leader. Jacques had escaped from a concentration camp in the final year of the war and joined the Maquis. He came to Brussels, and together we worked out a plan.

The Spaniards would come to Valenciennes on a Saturday, one by one. Jacques and his people would put them up overnight. On Sunday, the Jewish scouts would take their regular weekly hike through the woods between Valenciennes and Peruwelz, a Belgian border village a couple miles away. The boys and girls of Valenciennes were no strangers to the customs police in Peruwelz, where they often stopped to buy soft drinks, cookies and candy before returning to the French side. I would wait for the hikers with a small closed truck at the Peruwelz railroad station. Jacques was to have the Spanish sailors join the hiking youngsters in the woods, and when they reached the station, they would board my truck. Jacques assured me that I could depend on the youngsters.

We arranged telephone communications, passwords and recognition signals for the Peruwelz rendezvous. We informed Paris about our plan. I drove to Peruwelz, a lovely village which I explored for an hour in order to familiarize myself with the terrain. Willy took care of everything in Antwerp and alerted the shipping agent to expect the sailors. From our British Army surplus stock at Angen, a major Mossad center, I took a small Bedford truck. We covered the truck with a tarpaulin and installed seats for a dozen passengers.

I drove the truck to Peruwelz on the scheduled day and parked it behind the station about an hour before our 4 P.M. rendezvous. Few people were about. I had a snack at the lunch counter. The villagers were enjoying the usual nap after their hearty Sunday dinner, washed down by frothy beer in gigantic tankards. Just before four o'clock the village brass band began its weekly concert in a nearby park. Most of the customs officials and border guards were members of the band, which was why we had chosen this hour for our operation. The stolid citizens of Peruwelz slowly emerged from their homes and dutifully surrounded the band. The chords of marches and waltzes resounded loudly.

Four o'clock came. I glanced toward the woods, separated from the station by a green meadow. At 4:05 I detected movement at the edge of the woods, and about thirty figures emerged, holding hands and swaying from side to side in a gay dance. The boys and girls were wearing scout uniforms and gay kerchiefs. I looked more closely and caught my breath. Swaying heavily between every boy-girl couple was a Spaniard. It was impossible to mistake them. Most of them were over forty. Their faces were lined and weatherworn. Incredibly, one was lame and another wore a black patch over one eye—classical pirate images. They wore rough blue or gray overalls and faded sailor caps or large Basque berets. On their shoulders they carried duffle bags or sea chests, despite our strict orders to the contrary.

The spirited youngsters were singing cheerful scouting tunes and swinging the arms of their lumbering charges up and down and left and right, so that no one should suspect that they did not belong to the group. I broke out into a clammy sweat. One glance from a border guard could ruin the entire operation. The band played on. I prayed for good music and a miracle, and opened the tarpaulin just in time to let the breathless Spaniards pile into the truck, with an encouraging *avanti* on my part. I jumped into my seat, not even pausing to thank the plucky Jewish scouts of Valenciennes. I started the motor and pressed down on the accelerator. As I drove away, I could hear the scouts launching into a new song.

I didn't stop until I reached the suburbs of Antwerp, three hours later. I drew up at a small restaurant and called the shipping agent. Willy was waiting with him, and soon I transferred my cargo to him. A few days later we received word from Sweden that the Spanish seamen were already aboard the three vessels, preparing for their voyage south.

The Royal Monceau

I WAS recalled to Paris, where Shaul had his headquarters. With the escalation of the struggle against the British on the issue of immigration and the expansion of Mossad operations, Paris had become our most important center.

Our quarters were at 5 rue Chabagne, a small street whose only claim to fame was that one of the most splendid bagnios in Paris had been located there, catering to the world's great. It was rumored that when Edward VII of England was still Prince of Wales, he found a haven here from his mother Queen Victoria, who ruled him as well as half the world. The house was now closed, but the aged concierge loved to reminisce about the "good old days" when the Russian royalty, American millionaires, Hungarian barons and Turkish pashas sought refreshing entertainment there before returning to their burdens of affairs of state or commerce.

Our staff was quartered in a few small rooms, camouflaged as a non-existent shipping company. We worked feverishly. Shaul divided his time between our office and his own hotel, directing the widespread network we had created across all of Europe and the Middle East and reaching to the United States.

From this headquarters went orders to the escape organizers who funnelled hundreds of thousands of Jews from Russia, Poland and other eastern European lands to central Europe and to south European shores, where they were turned over to the blockade-runners. Here also were planned the procurement and outfitting of ships, and contacts between the various branches and Eretz-Yisrael were coordinated. Here, too, was the financial center, which oiled the wheels of all this complicated machinery.

Shaul's hotel, which he used in order to reduce the risk, was the "Metropole," a modest establishment off L'Etoile. I often wondered what the hotel proprietors thought of this guest, who lived in a small room, dressed simply, spoke quietly and ate sparingly, yet who received an incessant stream of officers in all kinds of uniforms and strange characters from the east and west and who placed urgent telephone calls daily to New York, London, Warsaw, Milan, Genoa, Bucharest and Athens.

Routine matters were handled at headquarters by Ehud Avriel, whose talent for negotiation, whether with Jews or others, for extricating us from awkward situations, for quiet diplomacy on all levels, for rapid improvisation, were evident even then. Moshe Carmil—the *Moshe'le* to whom I reported when I joined the Mossad—was a sort of "traveling salesman" between Tel Aviv, Paris and the other branches.

Our offices hummed with activity. Day and night we were on the telephone with half the world, on a multitude of subjects—Jews, trains, ships, smugglers, currency, procurements and purchases, fuel and spare parts, navigation instruments and, again and again, wandering Jews on land and sea. We had code names for each and every item, and at times the rigid secrecy and the multiplicity of terms created some confusion. A popular story in our circle told of conversation that was purported to have taken place between our people in Paris and Milan. The Parisians wanted the Italian branch to make an urgent delivery of fuel to a small vessel anchored at a southern French port, where there was a severe fuel shortage. In Italy we had some surplus, acquired from British and American military stores. The code name for the boat was *Grandma.*

"Hello," said Paris, "can we talk to Alon's [Yehuda Arazi's] men?"

"Go ahead," said Milan, "we hear you."

"Good. Here's the problem. Our Grandma is very ill. Do you hear us?"

"Yes. Your Grandma is very ill."

"Since Grandma is very ill we called a doctor who said that she could be saved if we immediately got some medicine which you have."

"Fine," said Alon's men, who began to understand. "What medicine do you want and how much?"

"Please send Grandma fifty tons of heavy crude oil without delay," Paris trumpeted.

Some of our people lived in the Royal Monceau Hotel, which once was—and will some day probably again be—quite respectable.

At that time, however, it teemed with all kinds of bizarre types—undercover agents, dealers in hard and soft currencies, dubious military officers, and similar characters who roamed Europe and dealt in all kinds of outlandish enterprises.

The hotel proprietors were not overly strict about the papers and identities of their guests or their standards of morality as long as they paid their bills on time. For a handsome tip, the waiters were prepared to do errands which were not listed in the *Guide Michelin* and which would not have earned it additional stars.

Another guest in this hotel was Meir Giron, our treasurer, who performed miracles in providing the huge sums we needed. He was a shrewd manipulator on the grand scale. In the grey and black money market, he traded hundreds of thousands of dollars ("Wises," in tribute to the great American Zionist leader, Dr. Stephen S. Wise), Swiss francs (called "horsemen,") and golden British sovereigns ("yellows"). Meir and his colleagues kept the wheels of the Mossad greased and spinning. His aide was Sarka, a fine talented young lady, who gained her expertise during her years of work with our Istanbul branch.

One evening, while working with Shaul in Paris, I received an urgent phone call from Meir at the Royal Monceau.

"Arthur," he said, "get over here fast. I've just learned that we've had an awful setback. I won't go into details now. The main point is that the inspectors of the Economic Department of the French Surete are on my trail. They may be here at the hotel any moment. I'm heading for Belgium. Get over here and take out the money cache."

"I'm on my way," I said.

Fifteen minutes later I was bounding up the hotel stairs to Meir's room. He was ready to leave at once. The money cache was above the big lighting fixture, which would have to be removed from its setting in the ceiling. Meir explained how this was done. The money was to be transferred immediately to Sarka, who lived on the other side of the town.

"One more thing," added Meir. "Take the keys to my De Soto. It's parked downstairs. Put the money sack into it and go straight on to Sarka." We said good-bye.

Above the fixture I found several million French francs, a few thousand dollars and a substantial number of gold coins. I quickly threw everything into a cloth sack, stuffed it into a small suitcase and left the hotel. Meir's long De Soto was standing at the curb. I unlocked the door, checked the glove compartment for the usual documents such as registration and insurance policy. Nothing there. I started the motor and drove down Champs Elysées to meet Sarka.

As I drove along the beautiful avenue between L'Etoile and the Place de la Concorde, the De Soto began sputtering and coughing. I pressed the accelerator, but the car did not respond. It slowed down. From its exhaust came what sounded like a death rattle. It rolled to a stop in the middle of the avenue. The fuel gauge's needle, I saw, pointed to "E"—"empty."

All around me horns began to blow as outraged drivers dodged and swerved past me. A moment later came the sound of a siren, and a heavy motorcycle shrieked to a halt beside me. A helmeted French traffic policeman in a smart uniform and with a pistol in his belt, dismounted and approached.

"Monsieur," he addressed me in French. "What do you think you are doing? You are blocking traffic, no, Monsieur? Your driver's license and car registration, if you please, Monsieur."

Fortunately I was wearing a khaki-like gabardine suit which resembled an army uniform. I replied in English:

"I'm on my way back from the American Army staff in Cologne, and ran out of gas."

The policeman didn't understand me, and I tried a more basic English.

"I American cfficer," I said, gesturing accordingly. "American officer from General Headquarters American Army Germany."

The policeman saluted. I pointed to the fuel gauge. "Machine no petrol. No benzine."

"Oui, oui," replied the policeman. *"J'ai compris. Un moment."*

He stepped out into the traffic, stopped the first taxi and asked the driver to siphon off a few liters of fuel from his tank and into mine. The driver obeyed without a murmur.

I started the De Soto. It began to show signs of life and then burst into a roar. The policeman stood politely off to one side to see whether the American would be courteous and appreciative of the aid extended by the cabbie and the French Republic. I took out a fistful of francs, added a few green dollars as befitted an affluent American officer, and thrust them into the cabbie's hands.

The cabbie smiled, bowed and with a loud "Merci" drove off, richer by a day's pay.

The policeman saluted and so did I. With a "Thank you, Monsieur, thank you very much," I left the scene.

Sarka opened the door, a bit surprised. I handed her the valise and she sorted its contents with her customary efficiency.

"Just a minute," I pleaded. "How about a glass of brandy, to restore my soul?"

Monte Carlo

I WAS ordered to leave Paris for Marseilles. Although Mossad's staff headquarters was in Paris, the main office for the French branch was in the southern port city. In charge of operations here was "Rudy" (Shmaryahu Zameret).

One would be hard put to it to find two personalities as dissimilar as Arazi and Zameret. Yehuda was urban; Shmaryahu was a farm settler, a lover of nature and the rural landscape. Yehuda was an extrovert; Shmaryahu was retiring and modest. When it came to "a way of life," Yehuda was a connoisseur of the good things of life and dressed carefully. Shmaryahu was ascetic in all his tastes and dressed simply. Yehuda was quick to make decisions, sometimes almost to the point of rashness. Shmaryahu weighed things carefully and made his decisions coolly. The men who served under them became infected, so to speak, with the characteristics of their respective superiors. Yehuda's headquarters functioned in the charged atmosphere of a Hassidic rabbi's court. Shmaryahu's staff worked in quieter and more egalitarian fashion.

When I arrived in Marseilles, Shmaryahu said:

"Your assignment is to acquaint yourself with conditions in Monte Carlo to see whether we can bring one of our immigration ships to the port or elsewhere in the bay. Yozhi will work with you."

Yozhi was already waiting for me in Monte Carlo. He had been there for two days, registered at the Grand Hotel de Paris under the name of Klarmann. I telephoned him, and he recognized my voice immediately. I identified myself as his good friend William van Groot, in town to join him for a good time. I asked him to reserve a room for me, and we arranged to meet in the lobby of the Grand Hotel at six the next evening.

I entered the hotel on schedule and saw Yozhi at the bar, toying with a glass of brandy. I tapped him lightly on the shoulder, and he turned his red head and said:

"Come have a drink."

Yozhi was about thirty, slender and rather pale, with lively black eyes. But his most prominent feature was his thick, curly, red hair. His head was like a ball of fire. During the war he had undergone all kinds of hell—concentration camps, escapes, various armies, combat, capture, and again camps and escapes. Of Polish origin, he had acquired a remarkable knack for languages. He could barely read French, Italian, German or English, but he spoke all four easily and competently. This talent had stood him in good stead during the war. But he had many others. He could forge documents. He had a highly developed skill in smuggling. He had a professional knowledge of all the channels and byways of Europe's post-war black market network. Yozhi's path crossed ours somewhere in France, and he served us unhesitatingly in any way we asked. He was a warm-hearted Jew. Although he evinced no desire to join the immigrants himself, he felt a strong fraternal bond with them. I had met Yozhi in Paris several times, and we had become quite friendly. Now I told him what information was wanted.

"Let's take it easy," he said. "I've been here for two days. The place is infested with all kinds of agents, spies, smugglers. First let's get our bearings. Tomorrow or the day after we'll find some way to get the information."

Yozhi suggested that we start by spending some money on cards and other games in the hotel's famous Casino that same evening. I registered, showered, and put on a beautiful black suit, white shirt and silver-gray tie. Yozhi was waiting for me downstairs, dressed to the nines. We spent an hour at dinner, then went up to the Casino. We sauntered a while among the gaming tables to get into the mood, then sat down to play.

Western Europe was still in the throes of crisis and poverty, subsisting on the mercies of the Americans. Monte Carlo had lost much of its pre-war glitter. The good old days had not yet returned, nor had the tourists. Most of the American troops were gone. In 1946 Monte Carlo was a meeting place and entertainment center for black marketeers, agents and speculators who profited from the disaster which had befallen the continent. At Monte Carlo they sought to be taken for millionaires and financiers, but they looked and sounded spurious.

After a few hours at the tables, we relaxed in easy chairs and planned our tour of the port area the next day. Yozhi suggested that we hire a motorboat and cruise around on a voyage of exploration. However, we needed some sort of cover. What would two men be doing in a motorboat by themselves all day long? Only arousing suspicion. On the other hand, no one would ask what two men were doing in a motorboat if there was a girl aboard.

"If we have to," said Yozhi, "we'll get a prostitute or two. There are enough of them hanging around the Casino. Sure it would be better if we could get hold of a more respectable article."

Our eyes wandered about the womenfolk in the place. Most of the women were either too old, too ugly or too wealthy for our needs. Then we spotted a young girl of about eighteen, blackhaired and pretty, who was obviously suffering from boredom while Papa and Mama were busy with the chips. Yozhi and I approached her table and soon introduced ourselves as two young Swiss businessmen in Monte Carlo for a bit of relaxation.

"Glad to meet you," the young lady said. "My name is Phyllis Cohen."

Gradually we pried Miss Cohen away from her parents. We led her to the nearby bar, had a drink or two, a dance or two, and went out for a walk in the delightfully cool evening, along the palm-lined promenade. We invited her to join us next day for a boat ride. She agreed with the eager enthusiasm of a maiden scorning her parents to seek adventure in the company of two strange young men.

The next day we rented a fast motorboat. Phyllis appeared in brief shorts and gossamer sailor's jersey. Yozhi and I also wore suitable sports clothes. While Yozhi toyed alternately with Phyllis and the motor, I checked the anchorages, piers and size of the ships and yachts moored alongside each. We left the small port and examined the coves in the area. Occasionally we went ashore, measured the depth, and asked questions, explaining to Phyllis and the others to whom we spoke that we owned a yacht of two hundred tons and were planning to bring it to Monte Carlo for a *really* good time.

By the end of this enjoyable day, we had what we wanted. I sealed the adventure with a hearty kiss on Phyllis' lips. Several hours later I reported to Rudy in Marseilles.

PART TWO
THE VOYAGE

The "Ulua"

LATE IN 1946 Shaul summoned me urgently to Basel, where the World Zionist Congress was in session. Shaul had moved his headquarters to this Swiss city, scene of the first Congress almost half a century earlier, in order to enlist political support and to raise funds with which to continue our immigration and blockade-running operations.

This was the first Zionist Congress after the European holocaust, and an atmosphere of tragedy hung over the sessions. The gathering also had its heroic aspect. Among the delegates were representatives of the partisans, the ghetto fighters, members of the Jewish units in the British forces and leaders of the underground struggle against the British in Palestine. On the floor political issues were debated, but many eyes were fixed on the balcony where scores of leaders of the "illegal" immigration and blockade-running operations were seated. They were easily distinguishable by their youth and their air of quiet but determined activism, as well as by their dress: the leather jackets and fur caps of our men from Poland, Rumania, Hungary, Czechoslovakia and Yugoslavia and assorted khaki "uniforms" of those from the shores of southern Italy, Greece and southern France. As we met old friends, we exchanged handshakes and warm embraces as well as experiences.

Shaul took me to his hotel room for a private talk.

"Let's live it up," he suggested with his own brand of humor. In Shaul's lexicon, living it up meant a glass of tea. Tea with Shaul was no simple ceremony. He liked to brew it carefully and serve it to his guests with festive air. As we were thus living it up, he began:

"In a few days a ship by the name of *Ulua* will be arriving at Marseilles from the United States, manned by American Jewish volunteers. In Marseilles she will be re-outfitted. She's an obsolete naval vessel, sturdily constructed. Mossad wants to send her to the most distant spot from which we have taken any refugees—Sweden."

Why was Shaul telling me this? I could feel my heart pounding, and a surge of excitement and pride swept over me.

"We are thinking of manning the ship with an enlarged crew," Shaul continued. "The long distance, the fact that it will be a winter voyage, the unusual point of departure—all these factors complicate the venture. We will have to work hard. Rudy is assigning three of his best Palyam men and 'Gideonites'. I want you to command the ship."

"Shaul," I said, "I thank you for your confidence in me. Who will be the captain and crew?"

In addition to the American seamen, there would be two of our naval officers, who had been assigned to our operation in the United States. The crew would be reinforced in Marseilles with several non-Jewish seamen.

"Rudy is working on this," Shaul said. "Meanwhile, stay here until the Congress is over. I need you here for consultations."

I spent about ten days in Basel. When I returned to Paris I purchased a large Alpine knapsack with many compartments, packed my few personal belongings and went to Marseilles to meet Rudy and the *Ulua*.

In Rudy's room I met "American Joe"—Joe Boxenbaum—whom I had known in Italy. He was one of the first Americans to join our operation; he became interested in our work while serving in Europe as an army officer during the war. When the war was over he volunteered for service with our American branch which had been charged with three tasks: fund-raising, acquiring ships and sending them to embarkation ports, and recruiting Jewish crews. Short of stature, energetic, with excellent contacts, Joe soon became one of the chief aides of Ze'ev Schind, director of the American branch, whose nom-de-guerre was "Danny". I had met Joe when he came to Italy to prepare the blockade-running *Wedgwood,* a corvette we had acquired from U.S. Navy surplus along with a sister-ship, later the blockade-runner *Haganah*.

"Arthur," said Rudy, "tonight the three of us will visit the *Ulua,* which is now in your command. Joe will tell you something about the ship and the Americans on board."

The *Ulua,* Joe told me, was about thirty-five years old, built before World War I for the U.S. Coast Guard. When the United States entered the war, she was armed with cannon and machine-guns and assigned to convoy escort duty, but returned to Coast Guard chores between the wars. In World War II she was again assigned to escort duty, but spent most of the war years gathering meteorological data in the North Atlantic and the Arctic Ocean. After the war, she was sold to a South American firm which converted her into a freighter, carrying fruit, chiefly bananas, from Central America and the Caribbean.

Danny and Joe first saw the *Ulua* while in Florida on a bargain-hunting mission for us, and fell in love with her the moment they set eyes on her. They had been looking for just that type of ship, a former combat vessel of several hundred tons. With the aid of Jewish friends, they were introduced to a young attorney, Dr. Jorge Fidel Doron of Tegucigalpa, capital of Honduras, who helped them with the financial and other formalities involved in purchasing the vessel. The name *Ulua* was borrowed from a river in the Republic of Honduras. (The Honduran flag, by coincidence, has alternating blue and white stripes.) Doron and his friends also saw to it that the *Ulua's* crew was furnished with legal Honduran seamen's certificates. These were large and impressive, and bore a Naval Ministry inscription in gigantic letters as well as the engraved seal of the Republic.

"The crew," said Joe, "is a rare mixture, ranging from ex-Marines to men who have never even smelled the sea. We were lucky enough to get three officers, two of your men and one American, real professionals. The ship's code name will be *Yuval*. She can carry up to two thousand passengers."

Each of our ships had at least three names: the original one under which she was registered in her home port, the Mossad code name she bore until she sailed, and the name given her as she sailed for Eretz-Yisrael—or, sometimes, when she was already at sea. These final names, beginning with the *Haganah,* were chosen to honor an event, person or concept associated with our cause.

That evening Rudy drove us to the ancient wharves of the port of Marseilles, and parked near the shipyard where the *Ulua* was being put in shape.

"There she is," Rudy said.

The *Ulua* was bathed in floodlights. The work on her had been pressed day and night. Sparks and flashes spurted along the ship and illuminated the figures of the welders hunched over her deck. She was a small gray ship of about seven hundred tons, with a sharp bow. A tall mast topped her command bridge. She had a single smokestack amidships. Astern, where torpedoes and depth charges had once been stored, the French shipyard workers were now toiling to build an additional deck, which ruined the ship's military silhouette and gave her an odd appearance.

We mounted the gangplank. A muscular young guard greeted us with a resounding American "Hi!" On the bridge a group of people awaited us. I recognized a few of them.

"This is Arthur," Rudy introduced me, "and these are Gad, Uzi, Miri, Nissan, Ephraim and Musik." To a man standing near Gad, he said in English, "Art, meet Arthur." I knew Uzi and Miri well, having worked with them in our Italian branch. Both were members of the first contingent of Palyam seamen who had worked in Italy with Yehuda Arazi. Both had already commanded ships running the blockade. Uzi was very young, and his slimness made him look even younger, but he was energetic and capable. His eyes and curly hair were black. Miri, on the other hand, was solidly built, broad of shoulder and deep of chest, his face adorned with a mighty Hussar's mustache, and thick eyebrows curling above an eagle's beak of a nose. Despite his belligerent appearance he was always amiable, hard-working and ready for any task, large or small.

I had never met the others from my own country. Gad and Ephraim had boarded the *Ulua* in the United States and brought her to Marseilles, Gad as captain and Ephraim as chief engineer. Both volunteered for Aliya Bet not from the ranks of the Mossad or Palmach but directly from service in the merchant marine. Despite his youth Gad was a certified, experienced deck officer. He had left his Haifa home as a young boy and climbed steadily up the ladder of marine rank. During the war he sailed the seven seas with the British merchant fleet, underwent baptisms of fire and water and became, in his middle twenties, an excellent mariner. Ephraim, short and slim, the same age as Gad, had been a mechanic since boyhood and already had a long career in engine-rooms. He had a level-headed, deliberate way about him. Nissan, the third of the Palyam men aboard, was younger than Uzi and Miri and had only recently come to Europe. He impressed me as being wise and courageous, with a sharp, dry sense of humor. Musik, our "Gideonite" and the youngest among us, had recently completed his training back home as a radio operator. This was his first assignment to the dream of every "Gideonite" —blockade-running duty.

That first evening and the next day I also got to know our American crew, a varied group of twelve Jews. Three of them, headed by Art Bernstein, were ex-U.S. Navy men. Art—tall, black-haired, as handsome as a Hollywood matinee idol—had the rank and papers of a First Officer. Four others were former U.S. Marines who had seen service in Europe and the Far East; their experience was in combat rather than at sea. The others were young Jews who had caught our "fire" and answered the call for volunteers to serve on blockade-runners, some because of their upbringing in Jewish homes or orientation in the American Zionist youth movement and others because they were impelled by a newly-awakened sense of peoplehood. These men had not known each other previously, but the Atlantic crossing had welded them into a unified crew. It was not an easy process. Most of them were not seamen and were unfamiliar with deck duties or ship's machinery. Gad, Art and Ephraim had to use all their powers of persuasion to get them to accept ship's routine. Now that we were joined by more of our men whose duties were not clear to the Americans, the issues of rank and command became my first problem. To complicate matters still more, Rudy and his branch staff decided to add to our crew five non-Jews, an officer and four experienced seamen.

Captain Pedro Lopez, a veteran captain of about fifty, was a Spanish Republican who had been living as an exile in Marseilles for more than ten years. The four seamen with him were also Spanish exiles. He had a square, grim, sad face. As for the men, years of toil at sea and, perhaps even more, the long hopeless years in exile had left their mark on them. They were known to our French branch to be disciplined men who could be trusted to do their work well.

The *Ulua*'s crew bore two aspects—an external-formal one and an internal-Mossad one. To outward appearances Art was the captain and Gad and Lopez were his assistants. I was purser and the Dutch passport issued to me by our Documentation Department in Paris was in the name of William van Groot. Ephraim was the chief engineer, one of the Americans was boatswain, and all the rest—Americans, our men and Spaniards—were listed as deck hands and engine-room workers. In reality, and to all practical purposes, Gad was the captain and Art and Lopez were his assistants. The three Palyam seamen were to be in charge of the refugees when the latter came aboard, and would assist Gad throughout the operation. I was responsible to the Mossad for the entire ship and her voyage.

Palyam seamen usually commanded our ships, and it was only in special cases, such as the *Ulua,* that a Mossad man who was not a seaman was placed in command.

The ensuing weeks passed in feverish preparations for the voyage to Sweden. In the French shipyards all partitions were ripped out below decks and all superfluous equipment was removed. Officers' and crew's mess rooms were dismantled to gain every possible inch. In the space thus created, we constructed five or six tiers of long planks, dividing them into bunks about five and a half feet long and sixteen inches wide, with about eighteen inches high and aisles less than two feet wide. We divided the ship's belly into blocks. Block A was forward, Block B amidships, Block C stern. On the afterdeck we built Block D. Altogether, we provided sleeping space for about a thousand people. We also enlarged the kitchen and installed large cooking cauldrons which, using the ship's steam, could prepare food for a thousand people at a time. We built a dozen showers and two dozen toilets. The *Ulua* had been stocked with food back in the United States, especially canned meat and fruit. In France, we added sugar, cheese, powdered milk and eggs.

Our plan was to take about a thousand refugees aboard in Sweden, sail them to the Mediterranean and at a point near Cyprus transfer them to a wooden vessel of about a hundred tons which would take them to Eretz-Yisrael. We would sail the *Ulua* back to Italy or Yugoslavia, take on another thousand and repeat the process. We had carried out similar operations during the past year. The chances of reaching shore without detection by British planes and destroyers were growing steadily poorer. The Mossad was reluctant to lose its strong, swift ships, and the *Ulua,* a former naval vessel and capable of developing a speed of thirteen knots, was considered to be one of the finest ships in our fleet. She had a cruising range of a thousand miles, far too short for us as the journey from Sweden to Eretz-Yisrael was three times that distance and we preferred not to stop anywhere to refuel. The shipyard workers therefore constructed three large fuel tanks on the forward deck. With this fuel, and the drums of fuel stored in the hold, the *Ulua* could sail all the way from Sweden home, although with little to spare. The large tanks forward and the superstructure astern for the refugees completely altered the ship's silhouette and transformed her into a strange-looking vessel indeed.

We supplemented the ship's life-saving equipment and installed boats, rafts and lifebelts for about two thousand people. We brought aboard a powerful radio transmitter and receiver, and Musik was entrusted with its installation. In a seamen's store in a Marseilles alley, we bought dress uniforms befitting Honduran seamen: shining gold buttons with anchors, broad gilt sleeve-stripes, and officers' caps embroidered with gold braid, silver stripes and an assortment of stars. I grew a long mustache. With my impressive headgear I felt I could pass for a naval officer.

Our departure date for Sweden drew near; we were supplied with collective Cuban visas obtained by our people from the Cuban vice-consul in Paris. These visas certified that "the individuals listed below"—and here a number of pages were left blank, to be filled in with the names of the refugees—"are traveling to Cuba for purposes of rehabilitation and resettlement."

That year Europe had a severe winter. Marseilles was repeatedly blanketed with snow, and the port was battered by heavy winds and bitter cold. We lived aboard the *Ulua,* kept warm and slowly got to know each other. The crew began to shape up. On December 31 we received orders from Paris to sail for the North Sea. Our destination was the port of Trelleborg in the south of Sweden, where we were to take aboard about a thousand refugees, most of them women. Our contacts in Sweden would be Ben-Nun and Avishai. We would receive further instructions en route. Our radio contact would be with headquarters in Paris.

We spent New Year's Eve on board together with the people from the Marseilles branch of Mossad, including Rudy. He gave me a considerable sum of money—dollars, pounds sterling and British gold sovereigns—and two pistols. I deposited all this in the ship's safe in the captain's room. We filled our glasses and drank a toast: "To our ships at sea." At midnight the church bells of Marseilles rang out the old year and rang in the new and ships in the harbor blew their whistles, all as though in salute to us. We took leave of our friends and weighed anchor, and at dawn on January 1, 1947, we were well out of Marseilles harbor, heading southwest toward Gibraltar, where we would turn north.

Copenhagen

We were in the North Sea, sailing up the Danish coast toward Sweden. About a hundred and fifty miles from Copenhagen, as Musik was listening to a weather report, broadcast by a coastal radio station, he picked up the news that the harbors of southern Sweden were frozen in. We hoped at first that this was a temporary condition, but the report was repeated constantly and ships heading for Sweden were advised to put in at Hull and Aberdeen in Great Britain or at Copenhagen in Denmark.

We advised headquarters in Paris of this unexpected blow to our carefully planned schedule and asked for instructions. Paris got in touch with our people in Stockholm and the operation in Sweden was temporarily halted, the passengers being asked to stand by. We were instructed to enter Copenhagen, which we welcomed, as we were reluctant to waste even one drop of our precious fuel.

We approached Copenhagen's large and busy harbor on a cold, gray morning and were greeted by a motor launch of the Danish Royal Navy. The young officer aboard examined us at close quarters. He had good cause for wonder. Aside from our bizarre appearance, we had entered the harbor without advance notice. He may have thought that we were a Honduran training vessel on its way to pay a courtesy call in Denmark and had simply forgotten to notify the fleet duty officer. At any rate, he ordered a few salute banners to be run up his mast. We replied with a civilian salute, to avoid any mistake. As soon as the officer realized that he was dealing with a civilian craft, he hailed us through his megaphone:

"Where are you from? What are you doing in Copenhagen?"

We replied:

"This is a freighter on its way to Sweden. The harbors are frozen in there, and we need shelter for a few days."

"O.K.," he replied.

"We have nothing to load or unload in Copenhagen," we continued. "Our funds are low. We don't want to tie up at a pier. We should like to tie up at the edge of the port."

"Right. I'll find out where we have mooring space available. Wait here until I let you know."

Soon a pilot came aboard and steered the ship to an anchorage on the far side of the port. Satisfied, we tied up at a floating buoy. Everything was going well. We were out of harm's way. All we had to do was to be patient until the frozen waters of Trelleborg thawed out.

Our peace of mind did not endure for long. Several hours later a motor launch of the port authority drew up and a junior officer asked permission to come aboard. We lowered a rope ladder. He had some blank forms he wanted us to fill out. On the bridge were Captain Art, First Officer Gad and I, the purser, all three of us in our officers' uniforms. We invited the Dane to come up on the bridge and offered him some excellent French cognac from the small bar in the captain's cabin. We chatted about all sorts of things—the frozen harbors in Sweden, the weather, the quality of our brandy.

A few glasses later we asked him about the forms. Now in a jovial mood, he explained that the forms were a matter of routine and that his superiors had ordered him to have us fill them out completely and to find out what he could about us. We studied the forms. They called for information on the boat's destination, its ownership, cargo and other details. We expressed our astonishment at this unusual routine.

"Sorry," said the officer. He took his leave and returned to his launch. Soon it returned with a higher-ranking officer aboard. We were not too happy about it, but there was no choice. The officer came aboard and asked, with crisp courtesy, to be shown around. We invited him to see the captain's cabin, but no, he wanted to see the interior of the ship first. As we appeared to take offense, the officer relented and came up on the bridge. After a few drinks of the same French cognac, our visitor thawed out a bit, produced more forms and announced that he had to have a list of the entire crew—captain, deck officers, engineers, boatswain and seamen. He wanted all personal details such as name, place of birth, nationality. Something was indeed rotten in the state of Denmark. We expressed our amazement at such an unusual procedure toward a foreign ship seeking shelter from ice and wanting to tie up at the edge of the harbor for a few days. Mellow with cognac, he replied:

"Gentlemen, believe me, I thought it rather strange myself, but these were the orders I received from my superiors, and let me tell you—my superiors have their orders to keep an eye on your ship."

The tall Dane leaned forward and whispered confidentially:

"You know, it's being said—and please don't hold it against me for repeating it—that you are engaged in white slavery for South America . . . "

We gasped. We told him that he was completely wrong. We were no more than a crew of seamen transporting a ship from Marseilles to its Swedish proprietors to earn a few dollars.

"But, gentlemen," protested the officer, "agents of Lloyd's themselves gave this information to the Danish authorities!"

The picture was now clear. The Lloyd's people, who also served the intelligence apparatus of the British Navy, had probably identified us and divined our purpose. Lloyd's keeps track of the movements of all ships, from all ports, practically all over the world. They had doubtless detected us when we left Marseilles. As soon as we appeared in Copenhagen, the British applied pressure on the Danes to inconvenience us. The story about our being white slavers seemed consistent with the facts. Our visas were for Cuba, and most of our passengers would be girls. We had no choice but to fill out the forms as requested by the Danish authorities. We included only those crew members who had proper documents—the American volunteers, Gad and Ephraim (Honduran seamen's cards), the Spanish sailors (rather dubious French identity cards) and I, with a Dutch passport. Uzi, Miri, Nissan and Musik were omitted; their documents were next to worthless. The officer left, leaving us in a mood of apprehension. Nor was this groundless, for soon the motor launch again drew alongside. A still higher-ranking officer, and a new demand: he wanted to inspect the crew. How about going up to the captain's cabin for a drink? No, his orders were that we were to parade the crew. We displayed some irritation. *Nothing doing, sir. We're not your nationals and we are not going to hold any kind of parade. We further wish to lodge a strong protest against this shameful treatment. Is this your manner of treating guests? If you want us to leave your port and head out to sea, say so frankly, but stop harassing us. It does you no honor.*

The officer wavered between embarrassment and irritation. *Very well, gentlemen, I shall return to the harbor authorities and report that you refuse to parade your crew for inspection.* He left, and we awaited further developments. They came soon in the form of an impressive, white motor launch, flying a large Danish flag at its stern. Its officers' caps were decorated with gold and silver braid and the insignia of high rank. This, we knew, would be the showdown—and, indeed, it was.

"The commandant of the Port of Copenhagen asks permission to come aboard with his aides."

We immediately lowered the gangplank. The first to come up was a tall, erect Dane, white-haired, with steely blue eyes and stately bearing. He was followed by five senior officers and several juniors. The commandant introduced himself and said:

"I should like to inspect your ship. We have no intention of disturbing your voyage. However, as you are within the limits of the harbor of Copenhagen, it is my right to inspect the ship and it is your obligation to allow me to do this."

We perceived that, this time, our French cognac would be of no avail.

"Gentlemen," I said, "please follow me."

I took them to the *Ulua*'s hold. The Danish officers stood near me, apparently cool and indifferent. However, I thought I detected a spark of curiosity at the strange sight that greeted them—hundreds and hundreds of wooden bunks in five tiers, each marked in red with a serial number. At one end were signs in Hebrew: KITCHEN—TOILETS—WATER STATION.

Slowly we filed along the narrow aisles, past the tall wooden structures. Our guests peered right and left. The commandant's retinue followed several paces behind us, apparently at his orders. He and I began to chat. He said:

"I beg your pardon, sir, but I didn't get your name. Would you please repeat it?"

"Certainly," I said, "van Groot."

"You are from Holland?"

"Yes, I am Dutch."

"And what are your duties on this ship?"

"I am the administrative officer, sir."

"You are a mariner?"

"No, I am studying in France. This is just a temporary job."

"And how about the other members of the crew? Where are they from?"

"It's a mixed crew. There are some Americans, some Spaniards, some Hondurans."

"The crew boarded the ship in Marseilles?"

"That's correct. The crew was put together in Marseilles and the men are to sail the ship to Sweden."

"May I ask what you intend doing with the ship once you get to Sweden?"

"I don't know. We're a transit crew. We are being paid to bring the ship from Marseilles and hand it over to a shipping company's agent in Sweden. We really have no idea what will be done with it there."

"I understand," said the commandant. "You know, I keep looking at you and your fellow-officers and I get the impression that you are all intelligent young men. Has the simple thought ever occurred to you, Mr. van Groot, that you are transporting a very strange ship? What are the queer structures on deck? Why are there large tanks forward? And above all, what are these hundreds of shelves here, and the red numbers? What is all this? What is the purpose of this ship, which you are merely transporting from Marseilles to Sweden?"

I shrugged. "I have already told you, sir. I don't know. It's none of our business. All we're interested in is to earn a few dollars by transporting the ship. We don't care what's done with her once we get her to her destination."

The commandant turned his penetrating gaze on me, but I saw not the slightest trace of animosity in his eyes. "Mr. van Groot, you certainly must have given some thought to the nature of this ship. Please tell me what conclusions you have come to."

I realized I could no longer avoid a direct answer and decided to reveal my "conclusions."

"I assume that the ship will go to a company conducting research in distant fishing grounds, possibly near the North Pole. On these shelves the fishermen and researchers might place water tanks, like aquariums, to sort and classify the fish they catch. The containers would be marked with the same red serial numbers."

The Danish officer hesitated, as though carefully weighing my theory.

"That's a plausible possibility—a research ship in the North Atlantic and around the North Pole. Hmm." He bent closer, looked me straight in the eye, and asked, almost in a whisper: "And how much are the Jews of New York paying for this fishing expedition,

Mr. van Groot?"

I was taken aback but tried to maintain control. "Sir, I have no idea what you are talking about."

The Dane straightened up. "I said nothing. Forget it."

We continued our tour of the ship. We passed through the long corridors, went by the kitchens (which could visibly feed hundreds of people), the toilets and the showers. We went back to the command bridge and with mixed emotions invited our guests to the captain's cabin for a glass of French cognac. The invitation was readily accepted. There were no further remarks about the ship and its mysterious mission.

My brain whirled feverishly. The Copenhagen port commandant obviously knew who we were and what we were doing. But what would be his next step? He might order us to leave port at once, which would not be disastrous. On the other hand, he might order our detention to appease British pressure on the Danish Government. At this point, the commandant asked if he could speak to me in private. "Of course," I said.

The others left the cabin and the two of us were alone. The Dane fixed his blue eyes on me and said, with the hint of a smile playing nebulously about the corners of his mouth:

"Mr. van Groot—or whatever your name may be; I doubt that it's van Groot, seeing that you are from Palestine—well, Mr. van Groot, listen carefully to what I have to say to you. Your ship was bought by American Jews and delivered to Palestinian Jews in order to transport as many as possible of the Jewish refugees now in Sweden. You are part of a fleet of illegal ships now on their way to Palestine. The British are after you with everything they have, and they are trying to keep track of your ships in every port in Europe and of your movements elsewhere. The British have been in Denmark since the war and still maintain military bases here. We are grateful to them for having liberated us from the Germans. They wield a great deal of influence in Copenhagen. As soon as you entered the harbor, they began pressuring us to harass you as much as we could, perhaps even detain you. We had no authority to do this, but under heavy pressure we agreed to inspect and interrogate you. I know that you are on your way to Trelleborg to load your little ship with hundreds of young Jews who found refuge in neutral Sweden from the Nazi terror. Mr. van Groot, I am now the commandant of the Port of Copenhagen, and I am carrying out the orders given by my superiors, but I want you to know where I stand in the matter in which you are engaged. Only three or four years ago I was a member of the Danish underground which operated against the German conquerors of our country. One of our most successful exploits was the evacuation to Sweden, by fishing boats, of thousands of Danish and other Jews. Our people performed this rescue work with devotion and enthusiasm, and some of them fell into the hands of the Germans in the course of this operation. I was one of the coordinators of this undertaking and I am happy to have taken part in this great humane act. Many of the Jews who will be boarding your ship on their way to their new homeland will be the same ones I and my companions brought to Sweden. They are wonderful people. Take good care of them and do everything to bring them home safely."

The Dane delivered himself of this long speech in slow, measured sentences, without letting his eyes leave my face for a moment.

"Commandant," I said, " I want to thank you, in the name of my comrades and for myself. We'll do our best."

"Well, we have talked long enough," said the commandant. "I have information that the waters in Trelleborg harbor will thaw within two days, and you will be able to enter. Until then, you can stay here safely. You will not be bothered again. I shall ask you not to let your men go ashore, as the British may make more trouble." He thought for a moment. "Are you well equipped for the long voyage? Do you have enough food and fuel? You may want to use your stay here for replenishing your supplies."

I made a quick computation. "Of course, Commandant, we used up a good deal of fuel coming here from Marseilles. We also need more food. We'd appreciate your help."

"How will you make payment?" he wanted to know.

"We have it in cash—dollars."

"Fine. A dependable agent will visit you today, with my warmest recommendations. He will try to get you everything you need."

I opened the door and the others came in. We had another drink, and shook hands, cordially, vigorously. We saluted and they left. Two hours later a jolly, fat Dane came bouncing aboard, and from that moment the cloud of our worries lifted. The next day a neat, fully-loaded tug tied up alongside and filled our fuel tanks. Then came crates of tasty Danish cheese, fresh Danish butter, good Danish biscuits.

The Danish commandant was correct in every detail. Two days later it was announced that the harbors of southern Sweden were open to shipping. We weighed anchor and headed for Trelleborg.

Trelleborg

WE INFORMED our people in Paris and Stockholm that we were leaving Copenhagen for Trelleborg. Twenty-four hours later we were instructed to enter port toward evening and that a special train would reach the pier siding in the morning.

We neared Trelleborg at dusk. From a distance we saw the neat little buildings of the gray city and, towering above them, the triangular spire of the municipal hall.

Neutral Sweden had not suffered upheaval and war. It was not overrun by troops or inundated with masses of refugees fleeing fire and sword. Never were her foundations shaken or her laws, customs and traditions uprooted. The countries of Europe were in chaos. Millions were on the move, without passports or documents, in rags, clothed in the remnants of uniforms. Civilian authorities were overwhelmed by the more or less official military bodies which sprouted like mushrooms following a rainstorm, bearing names consisting of every possible combination of initials. Within this terrible anarchy, we labored to move hundreds of thousands of Jews thousands of miles. We smuggled them across borders. We put them aboard caravans of trucks and trains. We sailed ships and flew airplanes. We used numerous aliases and haunted the back roads of the continent.

None of this occurred in Sweden. Refugees entered and left legally. There was no call for bribery or devious schemes. We therefore intended to enter Trelleborg harbor openly and legally. All the required documents such as ship's certificate and seamen's cards were prepared in advance. We carried papers attesting that we had come to transport about a thousand persons from Trelleborg to Le Havre, where they would be transferred to an ocean liner for voyage to Cuba, for "rehabilitation and resettlement." We also had the collective visa permitting all the refugees from Sweden to enter Cuba.

We cleaned the *Ulua* until she sparkled. We swabbed down the decks. We burnished every piece of brass until it shone like the sun itself. We wanted to be taken for civilized people, not buccaneers. Nor did we neglect our personal look. Gad, Art, Ephraim and I—the officers—donned our finest uniforms. The sailors and the Palyam men also did the best they could, and wore armbands reading "MONITORS." None of the port or customs officials who came aboard for inspection would be able to say that the ship was not fit for human beings.

The Swedes knew all about the *Ulua.* Our people in Sweden had done yeoman work, political as well as organizational, aided by the devoted cooperation of several Jewish leaders who convinced the authorities of the justice of our cause. Still, the Swedes wished to see with their own eyes whether we were properly outfitted and organized for the trip. They came aboard and with the utmost courtesy and professional concern asked us to show them our navigational, fire-fighting and rescue equipment. They counted the life belts, rafts and lifeboats, checked our sand buckets and fire extinguishers. Hours later, about midnight, they informed us that they would clear the ship for a short voyage. The passengers would be allowed to embark the next day for the trip to Le Havre, "where an ocean liner will be waiting to take them to Cuba." All this was said by the Swedes in full seriousness, without the trace of a smile. They played out their role down to the last detail.

The next day was beautiful. The snow had tapered off and was now falling in lazy floating flakes. The wind was blowing a bit more sharply across white-clad Trelleborg, but this did not prevent the curious townspeople and reporters from crowding the pier for a look at the strange ship moored there and the events about to occur. Our special train—a locomotive and seven or eight cars—was due in at ten o'clock in the morning. At 9:59, with Swedish punctuality, the train hove into view and was shunted off to a siding on the pier. With an impressive grinding of brakes the train came to a halt near the *Ulua.*

Three men descended. I recognized two of them immediately. They were the coordinators of the operation in Sweden: "Ben-Nun" (Yehoshua Rabinowitz of Kibbutz Genossar) and "Avishai" (Avinoam Rosenfeld of Kibbutz Beit Hashitta). The third was Gunther Cohen, a Swedish Jew who had thrown himself into the rescue work and had a hand in every action undertaken by Sweden's Jewish community on behalf of European Jewry. They came up to the gangplank to discuss embarkation procedures with us, informed us that each of the refugees, most of whom were women, had two suitcases.

This was bad news. The suitcases would fill up the dormitories and jeopardize the entire operation. Passengers with suitcases were *not* the rule on blockade-runners. Only a knapsack was generally permitted, and even this did double duty as a pillow. But these people had tasted of Sweden's bounty. We asked Ben-Nun and Avishai to have the immigrants hand over their valises to our men as they boarded the ship so that the gangplank would not be too cluttered. We posted a squad of American seamen in the stern with orders to stow all the luggage in one of the empty holds.

The Swedish colonel who had commanded the special train and represented the authorities in the operation now came aboard. He introduced himself to us and surveyed our embarkation procedures.

In the throng which poured from the train the women by far outnumbered the men. The blockade-runners which sailed from the shores of Greece, France and Italy usually had twice as many men as women, the result of a rigorous selection policy based on physical fitness.

In Sweden the situation was entirely different. During the final stages of the war, several thousand young Jewish women reached Sweden from concentration camps. Toward the end of the war, as the dimensions of the carnage became known, Sweden's Red Cross made desperate efforts to save Jews, and the more daring Jewish leaders in Sweden took part in this effort. Contact was established with Gestapo leaders, even with Himmler himself, who hoped that an act of charity would save him from retribution at the hands of the victors who were tightening the noose of steel and fire around Germany from east and west. A few months before the war's end, therefore, the Gestapo leaders agreed to hand over to Sweden several thousand girls still languishing in concentration camps. From Auschwitz, Bergen-Belsen and other camps, trains full of women and girls suddenly began to move. They had no idea where they were being taken, and hence were indifferent to what was taking place, many of them looking forward to death as a release. The trains moved north, and the astonished women sensed that this was not the usual death ride. They were transferred to large ferries and much to their amazement soon found themselves in Sweden, treated with great compassion by the people of the Red Cross. Their meeting with other Jews was a traumatic experience. They saw Jews who were well dressed, well fed, secure, crowding together at the quarantine fences to welcome them with cries of *shalom aleichem* (welcome), weeping bitterly at the sight of the newcomers—ill, hungry, emaciated, in tatters.

The Jewish women were indeed in poor health. The long years in the camps had left their mark. The women suffered from typhoid, tuberculosis, dysentery and other diseases. Sweden opened its finest hospitals and convalescent homes to them. The small Jewish community took the forlorn girls to its bosom. A year later, most of the girls had responded to the excellent treatment and had recovered completely. Youth asserted itself. Creatures of skin and bone blossomed into healthy, vivacious women. The Swedes gave them every opportunity to learn the language and to be trained as nurses, clerks, and in other skills. As they were stateless, they were given special Swedish passports, and in time would be able to become full-fledged Swedish citizens.

There were some men as well, mostly able-bodied young German Jews who had fled to Denmark before the war and there established Zionist pioneer training farms. When the Germans invaded Denmark, they escaped or were smuggled to Sweden, where they were joined by some young Danish and Swedish Jews and formed a nucleus of Zionist youth preparing for immigration to Eretz-Yisrael. They were helped in their work by emissaries we sent to Sweden in 1945 and 1946. As nature took its course, many of the concentration camp girls found their mates among the pioneer boys, but the number of couples was rather small. The excess of girls presented quite a problem in the Jewish youth clubs in Stockholm, Malmo and Trelleborg. Most of the girls came from religious Zionist homes. Many had relatives in Eretz-Yisrael who were urging strongly that they be brought there as quickly as possible. It was this pressure which brought the Mossad into the picture. As a result, we were now standing and gazing at the hundreds of de-training girls, all neatly dressed and carrying their own valises. They had evidently taken pains to look their festive best for the embarkation.

They were now informed that each of them would be assigned a bunk which they were not to leave until the ship was at sea, to reduce confusion to a minimum. All had been forewarned, by the Zionist emissaries and our Aliya Bet people, about conditions aboard ship, but reality spoke even more eloquently. The first girls entered cheerfully and occupied the bare wooden bunks, but soon the tiers became crowded. The ventilation system was not functioning well. Warm air stagnated in the dormitories. The laughter, banter and small talk died out and a heavy silence settled on the women.

The embarkation proceeded as planned. The women left their luggage with the seamen, mounted the gangplank and then followed the directions of the monitors to the blocks, where each quietly occupied the first cot available. There were several older couples. One elderly man entered a block and recoiled from the sight of the tiers and the figures stretched out in the bunks.

"No, no," he cried. "I won't go to another camp. I won't fall into the hands of the Gestapo again."

I gave orders for him to be taken ashore immediately, to avoid any impression that anyone was being coerced into boarding. The man and his family—a wife and daughter—returned to the pier and wept quietly as they saw the long line disappearing into the ship. I saw them go back to the train, convulsed with sobs. Yet when the ship was out in the open sea, there they were. At the very last moment they had decided there could be no going back, and they quietly joined the last of the passengers. This elderly man, a cabinet-maker, proved eventually to be one of the best, quietest and most devoted people aboard the *Ulua*.

By noon most of the people were aboard. We were still not organized to serve food in orderly fashion, and could only distribute tea from large buckets carried along the aisles between the bunks. By early afternoon, the train was empty and all were aboard. We wanted to weigh anchor and sail as quickly as possible, in order to clear the Straits of Skagerrak in daylight. Uppermost in our minds was the desire not to become involved any further with the Swedish authorities. We could think of a hundred possible complications. What if the Swedish colonel should go below and be upset by what he saw there? What if some passengers broke down and caused a commotion? Or unfavorable orders came from Stockholm? Perhaps the excitement stirred by the reporters would produce an undesirable reaction and our sailing be prohibited.

I approached the Swedish colonel, who had been standing near the gangplank all this time.

"Sir, we are ready," I said. "We ask permission to leave and we should like to have a pilot."

The colonel glanced at his watch. "Not yet," he said, in English.

I went back to the bridge.

A bit later, Gad tried it.

"Not yet," repeated the colonel.

We suddenly got the nervous feeling that we were becoming entangled in some kind of bureaucratic maze. I approached the colonel once again.

"Sir," I said, "I can't understand what is going on. Soon the sun will set. Why are you detaining us?"

"Sir," replied the colonel, "please be patient. The pilot will soon be here."

A staff car of the Swedish Navy drew up. A naval officer carrying a long cylinder got out and saluted the colonel, and the two exchanged a few words. The colonel then called Gad and me to his side and said:

"Gentlemen, this is a pilot of the Swedish Royal Navy. We have summoned him from the nearby naval base and asked him to bring the most recent maps of the minefields in the Straits of Skagerrak and Kattegat. As you know, those straits were mined during the war by all the belligerents, and they have not yet been cleared. We assign a civilian pilot to guide ordinary ships through the Straits. However, we know how precious is the human cargo you are carrying, and we thought it would be better if the Navy were your guide."

The pilot went up on the bridge and we weighed anchor. Most of our passengers, after hours inside the ship's belly, came out on deck and waved farewell to the land and the people who had given them shelter. Spontaneously the girls began to sing a Hebrew song. From the pier the Swedish sailors, stevedores and policemen waved farewell.

On shore, too, we could see Avishai, Ben-Nun and their companions waving to us. Their part in the operation was over; ours had begun. We now had about a thousand "illegal" immigrants. From now on we would be a warship of the Jewish navy bearing units of the Jewish people to the shores of the Land of Israel.

Skagerrak

At the end of the first day, I wrote in the ship's log:

"During the day we organized the assignment of bunks and selected group leaders. As a result of their stay in Sweden, these people are understandably unaccustomed to these conditions. Still, the first impression they make is generally very good. They are pleasant, intelligent and eager to be helpful. There is almost no need to raise one's voice to them. The sea is calm. In the evening the immigrants held a community sing. Lights out at ten."

The Swedish pilot had been dropped, and the *Ulua* was now in the open sea. The ship was entirely in our own hands. Gad and his crew—our men, Americans and Spaniards—were on duty on the bridge, on deck and in the engine-room. I could sense that as they performed their routine tasks every one of them was conscious of a tremendous responsibility, as though the life and fate of an entire Jewish community depended on him.

The ship hummed like a beehive. Busiest of all were our own men. The passengers had occupied the first bunks they found, without showing any preference as to location. Now many wanted to change bunks in order to be with old friends. A group of religious girls wanted to be with their leader, Ruhama. A Danish unit of *Hechalutz,* the pioneer youth movement, asked to be placed together in the same area. Girls who had lived near Goteborg wished to be near each other. It was almost like a population exchange. We armed ourselves with patience. Only a few persons at a time could file through the narrow aisles. Only in small groups could they ever go out on deck.

In the end, the rearrangement made things easier for us. We were now able to work with organized groups; we came to know their natural leaders and to avail ourselves of their help.

One group of German-born pioneers who had worked together on a *hachshara* (a preparatory training farm) in Denmark attracted our attention. Heini, Oshi, Ernst, Zvi, Margot, Slava and several other young men and women in their twenties had known each other for several years. Strong and lively, they looked more Nordic than the Nordics themselves—tall, rangy, mostly blond—one would hardly have taken them for Jews. This group had also brought the only child aboard. This was the pretty, two-year-old Nurit, daughter of Ernst and Margot, who immediately became the ship's darling. The *hachshara* men were skilled in many crafts, and they enthusiastically offered to share the responsibility for the blocks.

On the very first day we inquired about cooks, and there were many volunteers. Apparently anyone who had experienced life in the camps and ghettos became a master of the culinary arts. Yankel, a happy, energetic fellow, told us that he was "chief of chefs" in Polish and Russian military units before he fled across the Baltic to Sweden. More important, he *looked* like a head chef—and we were not proved wrong. Yankel picked his own staff and took efficient control of the cavernous kitchen. His soups were rich and tasty, and became our main daytime dish, ladled out of buckets by the monitors to each passenger at his own bunk. Yankel also knew how to keep an eye on the larder, wasted no food and kept his domain as clean as circumstances aboard ship allowed.

There was another remarkable group aboard—thirty young Bahad (religious pioneers) girls led by Ruhama. Most of the Bahad girls were survivors of Auschwitz, with tattooed numbers on their forearms. The pleasant years in Sweden had helped to obliterate, at least on the surface, the horrors of the extermination camp, and they were now in the full bloom of their feminine charm. Ruhama, herself but a few years older than her charges, supervised them firmly but lovingly. They listened to her attentively and obeyed her instructions. She spoke fluent Hebrew, acquired in a Jewish high school in Poland. Most of the girls had been born in Hungary and the rest in Czechoslovakia and Poland, and they hardly knew any Hebrew at all. Ruhama was a true leader and of invaluable assistance to us.

By the end of the first day, most of the passengers were more or less settled in the blocks they had chosen, and were prepared for the long voyage. We now turned our attention to those who had not found bunks when they came aboard and had been temporarily accommodated in the hold.

Tanya

AFT, IN the hold, several dozen women were crowded. There were no bunks, and the women had to bed down on the metal floor. During the day we were informed that water was seeping into the hold, and I took Nissan, Uzi and Ephraim down to investigate. The hold was in almost total darkness. A faint ray of light came down through the hatch, barely revealing the young women sitting or lying on the floor.

We were amazed to find them in good spirits. To them, this was an adventure within an adventure. They had been on deck for some fresh air and now they were entertaining their friends from the blocks and waiting patiently for instructions from "the authorities"—us.

We turned our powerful flashlights on the walls to locate the leaks, which we soon found to be more serious than we had expected. Thin rivulets of water were coursing down the walls, forming puddles on the floor. We would have to seal the cracks somehow and pump out the water already accumulated. First of all, however, we would have to remove the girls and find other quarters for them.

We discussed the situation freely among ourselves in Hebrew, assuming that the girls would not understand our "sabra" vernacular. We were therefore astounded to hear a feminine voice call out in clear flawless Hebrew:

"Friends, commanders, there's a leak here you haven't seen."

Our flashlights focused on the speaker, a young woman with a round face, button nose and charming smile.

"Another leak? Where?"

The young woman pointed to a puddle. We traced the leak.

"Add it to your list," I said to Ephraim. "We'll have to mark each one. Have Nissan and Uzi take all the women upstairs. As soon as the cracks are sealed we'll bring in the pump."

I was about to leave when I recalled the voice and the round face. I turned my flashlight in that direction.

"Where did you learn that Hebrew?" I asked.

"At home." She could not see the person with whom she was talking.

"Where was that?"

"In Kovno, Lithuania. I attended a Jewish high school."

My beam of light lingered a moment on the girl's face. "Fine," I said finally. "I understand. Tell your friends we'll be taking you out in a few minutes. Thanks."

"Thank you, friend," she answered.

We climbed up out of the hold. The girls were brought on deck and the block leaders had no difficulty finding bunks for them. A work gang went down to seal the leaks and pump out the water. By evening we were exhausted. Our men gathered in the captain's cabin, where we ate a hasty meal and discussed the long day. We joked fondly about the Swedes, our erudite passengers, our crew and even ourselves. Our talk flowed as freely as the water in the hold. It was midnight before we separated, in excellent spirits.

I laid my head on my pillow, and the events of the past two days flashed through my mind—the train, the Swedish officer, the immigrants, the ship dormitories filling with people, the wooden bunks, the delays, the pilot, the departure. And now the pace of the film slowed down: the hold, the rivulets of water, the image of the girl with the pretty face and the little nose. The image remained on my memory screen and would not yield to the next scene. "Friends . . . in Kovno . . . a Jewish high school . . ."

Who was she? Who was she? I was possessed by a strange impatience and curiosity. Sleep was out of the question. I got up, rinsed my face in cold water and put on a pair of seaman's overalls. In the next cabin was the ship's safe with our documents. Near it was a valise containing the hundreds of passports we had collected as our passengers boarded the ship. I opened the valise. The passports were there, in a tight heap. Large, red Swedish passports.

I began opening passports. Some hidden hope enticed me. Hers would be the third passport, or the tenth. Once I found it, I would calm down and go to sleep. I scrabbled hurriedly through a hundred passports without success. I saw that I must either work patiently and systematically or else forget all about what was obviously a queer caprice. I stacked the passports neatly, replaced them in the valise, and rose to go back to bed. But the image of her face again appeared in my imagination, and back I went to the valise.

This time, I calmly opened one passport after another. Hers, I assured myself, would be the very last. In the meantime I sorted the passports into two groups, men's and women's. If any of my comrades were to enter, I was putting things in order and sorting the passengers' documents by age and sex.

The piles of passports grew steadily. Finally I opened one, from which the girl's face looked into mine. A strange sense of serenity came over me. My eyes traveled slowly over the biographical data.

Family name: Zvi (rather odd). *Given name:* Tanya (what a wonderful sound). *Age:* 21. *Place of birth:* Kovno (Kaunas), Lithuania. *Height:* 5' 1" (petite). *Eyes:* Brown. *Hair:* Brown. *Occupation:* Children's nurse.

I replaced the passports, now arranged in exemplary fashion, in the valise. I took Tanya's with me. I undressed and slipped into bed. Several times I turned on the small bed-lamp to look at the photograph. Savoring the sound of her name, *Tanya, Tanya,* I fell asleep.

From the ship's log, January 25:

"Sea calm. Ship cutting through thin ice. Units organized to stand watch and for kitchen, sanitation and first-aid duty. Ship's routine established. This morning we held community prayers and read from the Torah. Passage from the Portion of the Week: *And he said unto them: 'Go, serve the Lord your God; but who are they that shall go?' And Moses said: 'We will go with our young and with our old, with our sons and with our daughters'* (Exodus 10, 8–9). And from Jeremiah 30, 10: *Therefore fear thou not, O Jacob my servant. . . , neither be dismayed, O Israel: for, lo, I will save thee from afar, and thy seed from the land of their captivity; and Jacob shall again be quiet and at ease, and none shall make him afraid.* The traditional blessings for the welfare of the ship, the captain, the passengers and crew were recited.

"Our passengers have brought quite a bit of sugar aboard, more than half a ton, as well as coffee, tea and canned butter. We have pooled all foodstuffs, which will help our food problem.

"In the evening we held an end-of-Sabbath gathering and a community sing.

"Snow fell during the night."

How adaptable people are, especially Jewish refugees. Forty-eight hours after boarding ship, our passengers were completely at home. In the morning they converted the sailors' mess into a temporary synagogue, read from the Torah while on the high seas, established regular meal schedules, went out on deck by groups in turn, all as though they had been doing it since time immemorial. The complete confidence they retained in us doubtless influenced them. We were very young men, unknown, bearing underground names. Nevertheless, they accepted our actions and instructions without question, fully convinced that we knew what we were doing and where we were taking them. Many of them volunteered for duty, the young men begging to be assigned to the bridge or the engine-room. Those we selected demonstrated adequate skills.

We asked for volunteer nurses to help our "doctor"—Jack, formerly a medical corpsman with the U.S. Marines. We had awarded him an "M.D." while preparing to take on the *Ulua* passengers and named him ship's doctor. Jack surrounded himself in the sick bay with a bevy of volunteer nurses, and examined their professional knowledge, conversing with them in a strange Brooklynese Yiddish. There were about half a dozen registered nurses, and our "doctor" couldn't have wished for a finer staff.

I watched Dr. Jack treat his first patients. His approach was professionally impeccable. He exuded medical authority. Every patient seeking his aid was given serious attention, although all received the same treatment. First came an expert thrust of a trusty thermometer into the patient's mouth. A glance, a frown, a knitted brow, and Dr. Jack ordered the nurse to give the patient a few aspirin tablets. Then the patient was cordially ushered out.

Another volunteer came forward to help Dr. Jack—Tanya. In broad daylight she appeared a bit different, smaller, almost diminutive. Her features were delicately carved, her eyes almond-shaped under slightly arched brows. Her Swedish ski jacket gave her figure a more rounded appearance. My heart beat strongly, and a warm wave of emotion suffused me. "What's the matter with you?" I chided myself. She smiled a greeting at me as she passed.

At night the people sat around in a close circle. An accordion, a harmonica and a guitar provided music. The singing was lively, rhythmic, a mixture of joy and sadness. They sang about their little towns, now wiped off the map, love ballads, Hassidic melodies, and songs of pioneering and the ancestral homeland that they learned in Jewish high schools in Poland and Lithuania. They sang the songs of the ghettos, the concentration camps, the partisan units, revolution. I drew near and scanned the girls, searching for Tanya. She was not among the singers. I found her at last, lying in one of the bunks, far from the circle of singers.

"Why aren't you with the others, Tanya?"

She raised her small, pretty head. She did not seem surprised to be addressed by name.

"I don't feel so well."

"Come, Tanya," I said. "Let's go on deck. It's cooler there, and you'll feel better."

Tanya rose. I helped her, and she leaned on my arm, simply, gently. We climbed to the deck. It was a cold night, flecked with snow-flakes. Despite her blue ski jacket and baggy ski pants, Tanya shivered slightly. I draped my pea jacket around her shoulders and drew her to me. We paced back and forth in a semi-embrace from one end of the deck to the other without exchanging a single word.

"How do you feel now, Tanya?" I said finally.

"Better, much better," she replied.

I took out a chocolate bar and broke off a section. "Want a piece, Tanya?" She nodded and lifted her face to me. I sank my teeth into the chocolate, bent down and brought it close to her lips. She laughed and bit into the other end.

Our lips met. The chocolate was broken off, but our lips lingered for a long moment.

"What's your name?" asked Tanya.

"Arthur."

"Arthur," repeated Tanya.

We went down the stairway and I led Tanya to her bunk. She pressed my hand, then lay down among the hundreds of others. I took my pea jacket and went back to the command room.

From the ship's log, January 26:

"Sea becoming stormy. Number of seasick rising. Held an emergency drill and taught passengers how to use life belts, how to reach safety exits, and other emergency procedures.

"Toward evening we discovered that ship's stability was defective. Weight of passengers—about fifty tons—pressing stern down, admitting water through vents of rudder lines. Organized a gang of sailors and passengers to bail water out with buckets. Others transferred luggage to bow. Engineers instructed to draw on the fuel and water in stern. Worked all night and restored ship's stability, but still needed constant relays to remove water. Basic solution would be to have pump working constantly. Ordered pump by radio."

The leaks occupied our entire attention. Moving passengers and luggage forward did not completely solve the problem. The water was no longer flooding in as before, but small streams were still entering the hold in the stern. To add to our troubles, the water got into one of our oil tanks and ruined its contents. Ephraim put the loss at two hundred barrels. He also announced that the packing in the high-pressure cylinder was faulty, causing a constant loss of steam pressure. We cabled headquarters in Paris about these mishaps, and reluctantly decided to put in at Le Havre for fuel, new packing and a pump.

We had no desire to court danger by entering port, even a friendly French port, with forged documents and loaded to overflowing with refugees. But we were compelled to weigh another consideration. The sea was becoming more and more turbulent, and we faced a difficult passage through the Bay of Biscay. We had no wish to enter the Bay without a pump and with a defective engine.

Le Havre

THE *Ulua* sailed slowly into the large harbor. We called for a pilot. Our decks were bare except for four or five sailors. Several officers were on the bridge.

The day before we had gathered all the block leaders and group leaders to announce that we would be putting in at a French port for a day or two. The ship must look like an ordinary merchantman. Nothing aboard was to give any hint of her true character. No one was to show himself on deck. The passengers were to remain below during the entire stay in port.

The announcement made the round quickly. No one complained.

The *Ulua* was moored to a large pier between an American Liberty ship and a bulky Norwegian freighter. The shipping agent we had sent for was known to us and was, in fact, associated with our organization. We listed our requirements: fuel, repairs, a pump. He asked no questions. He undertook first of all to arrange for a fuel barge to supply us. Oil was being rationed, and he had to move quickly to place our order. This done, he would attend to our other problems.

I was chatting with some of our men below when Uzi came running.

"Come to the bridge," he said. "Something funny is going on around us."

I jumped up and hurried after him, reaching the bridge within seconds. Gad, Art and Miri were there. Gad pointed to two tugboats of the port authority maneuvering in a strange manner alongside.

"What are they doing?" I asked.

"That's what I'd like to know," Gad replied. "It's very strange. We didn't ask for tugboats. Seems to me they're trying to block us. They haven't answered my questions."

The two tugboats suddenly looked to me like two sharks with murderous heads, which indeed was what they resembled with their disproportionately large bows. The boats were practically glued to us. We felt trapped between the pier and the tugboats.

"Ask them again what they want," I said.

Gad put the megaphone to his lips, leaned over the rail and shouted, in English, at the Frenchmen:

"What are you doing? Why are you blocking us?"

The French officers and seamen made no sign that they heard, and Gad repeated his question, this time in French. No reply.

We were still occupied with the movements of the French when Nissan came up on the bridge. "There are police trucks down below, on the pier."

Two truckloads of armed policemen leaped to the ground from their khaki-green vehicles and marched toward the ship in single file, then turned to face the ship in a long line. We were surrounded.

A Citroen pulled up at the gangway. A short Frenchman with a black goatee jumped out and rapidly mounted the stairway, followed by an aide and a sergeant. Without pausing on deck, the newcomer bounded up to us on the bridge. He drew himself up, breathing hard, and threw out his chest authoritatively:

"My name is Inspector LeBrun of the French Maritime Ministry responsible for safety aboard seagoing craft. I have been instructed to read to you the following notice."

The inspector hitched back his head and torso, and his well-trained assistant whipped out a document from his official-looking brief-case and handed it to him.

Our eyes were fixed on the bobbing pince-nez astride the Inspector's nose. Having completed his strident reading in French, he started to repeat its contents in broken English. The *Ulua* had entered the port of Le Havre with almost a thousand passengers. According to the best information available to him, the ship could accommodate no more than three hundred. We were therefore carrying more than three times the permitted number. For reasons of safety, the ship could not be given clearance to continue her voyage. As "inspector responsible to the Maritime Ministry of the French Republic" (he repeated the title with mounting emphasis) he had instructed the Le Havre port authority that we should not be permitted to sail.

Having delivered himself of this pronouncement, Inspector LeBrun turned on his heel. Before we could voice a word of protest he was already on the pier, climbing into his car.

We gathered in the command room for a feverish conference. We had to let Paris know about this immediately. We could never hope to untangle this knot by ourselves. Musik could not communicate by radio from a ship in port. It was against all international regulations and would provide the hostile port authority with even more ammunition. We decided to contact Paris by telephone.

Art, Bernstein and I donned our best Honduran uniforms, put on our braided caps, went down to the pier, and passed the gendarmes lined up like ghosts in the mist. We hailed a cab and gave the driver the address of our shipping agent. We found him wringing his hands, nervous, greatly distressed. Everyone already knew that orders had come from high quarters in Paris, from the Ministry itself, to prevent our departure. "What hard luck! What hard luck!" the agent lamented.

He permitted us to use his telephone and I called Mossad headquarters in Paris, whose number I knew by heart. Luckily, Ehud was in the office.

"Ehud, we're in trouble . . ."

"Ah, my dear Arthur," interrupted Ehud. "Glad to hear your voice. We know all about it. All this trouble started here yesterday. Old Satan himself took a hand in the matter and put pressure on the upper echelons of the Foreign Ministry, and they in turn ordered the Maritime Ministry to detain you. We're working day and night to marshal some influence on our side. Stand fast and do everything you can at your end. I'm sure that together, we'll pull you out of the mud." We exchanged information and coordinated our planning.

I asked the shipping agent about Inspector LeBrun, who had made such a show of authority. It appeared that the Inspector had greatly exaggerated his own importance. He was merely one of the junior inspectors in the Le Havre port branch of the Maritime Ministry. The Chief Inspector of the branch was a M. Douain, an elderly, highly respected man with considerable influence in Le Havre. We thanked the agent and cheered him up, telling him that he had nothing to worry about, that everything would turn out well, and that he would yet be supplying us with the fuel and equipment we needed.

We drove to the office of the Chief Inspector. M. Douain's pretty secretary favored us with a curious glance the moment she learned that the captain and the purser of the *Ulua* wished to see her boss most urgently. She went into an adjoining room, but soon returned and said:

"M. Douain will be glad to see you in a few moments."

"Thank you, Miss."

We sat down facing her. She was obviously wondering, "Are they really Hondurans?" Meanwhile, we observed that the legs of M. Douain's secretary, below her brief skirt, were very shapely.

The intercom buzzed, and the secretary asked us to enter the Chief Inspector's office. M. Douain was about sixty, with a shrewd look, wide forehead, penetrating eyes and neatly brushed silver-grey hair. He rose behind his massive desk and waved us to deep leather chairs. He spoke English, and Art Bernstein proceeded to state our case:

The *Ulua* is flying the flag of the Honduran Republic and is duly registered in Tegucigalpa. She has reached Le Havre that morning. Her several hundred passengers had embarked in Trelleborg with the permission of the Swedish authorities. Most of them are women, Jewish refugees on their way to settle in Cuba. They have Cuban visas. Our intention is to take them to their destination. We are in Le Havre only for refueling. We had been astounded to see port tugboats closing in on the ship and blocking her way. Also, policemen were stationed on the pier, as though we were criminals. This was an outrage, violating every concept of law and order. We are lodging a protest and demanding that the blockade be removed at once, permitting us to sail.

Inspector Douain listened patiently. He then opened a file folder lying on his table, extracted a sheaf of papers and said:

"I am most amazed that the Swedish authorities allowed you to sail under these conditions. Sweden is known for her strictness in all matters pertaining to regulations for machine safety. But this is for the Swedes to decide. Now that you have entered a French harbor, we cannot allow you to depart, since you are conveying passengers in a manner which endangers their safety."

I replied:

"Perhaps you will be good enough, M. Douain, to explain how we are endangering the safety of our passengers. If you are referring to the crowded conditions on board, I must admit the fact. Yet no one has ever drowned, nor has any ship ever capsized, merely because two or three times three hundred passengers were aboard. Congestion is a relative matter. If our passengers have agreed to travel in less comfort, that is their personal business."

"According to the documents I have here," said M. Douain, "you do not have sufficient safety measures."

My voice, when I replied, conveyed a trace of the outrage I felt. "Inspector, sir, the lives of the people we are transporting are no less precious—and are perhaps even a great deal more precious—than the lives of ordinary passengers aboard an ordinary ship. We have taken care to have all the rescue equipment required by law."

Douain gave us a long look. "I don't deny the first part of your assertion. However, I repeat that you are not properly equipped."

Bernstein took up the argument.

"Sir, the ship has six lifeboats capable of carrying an emergency load of about three hundred. We also have on deck three large life-rafts and eight small ones, enough to carry five hundred more. Together, they are enough for the number we have aboard. Also, every passenger has a life belt in working order, and we have seven hundred more in reserve. We have thirty-five life preservers. We have good fire-fighting equipment. The sailors are trained in rescue routines, and we have also put all the passengers through all the drills, as required."

Douain jotted something down on the paper before him. He leafed through the papers once more.

"Well," he said, "all that I can tell you now is that in accordance with my instructions you cannot leave port. Of course, I shall submit your version to my superiors."

"M. Inspector," I said, "let us put aside, for the moment, the legality—or, rather, illegality—of your attitude toward us. After all, we are asking for no more than your permission to leave. We are not asking for fuel, water or help—in short, nothing. You have force on your side. But I want you to know, M. Inspector, that our passengers are Jewish refugees who have experienced all the horrors of war and the extermination camps. They have become accustomed to resisting, not yielding to force." I looked him in the eye. "We have planned the trip to Genoa down to the last detail. We have calculated our fuel supply and our drinking water down to the last gallon, our food stocks to the last ounce. Each day, each hour, that you detain us here we are using up fuel, water and food. All this we shall need in the course of our voyage. We have instructed the crew, officers and men, and we also have the consent of the passengers, to stop the engines, turn off the electricity, close the kitchen and seal the food stores until you release us. I must inform you, furthermore, that the crew and passengers will resist with force any attempt on the part of your authorities to board the ship."

M. Douain raised his eyebrows.

"What you are telling me is that you are preparing to declare a hunger strike?"

"Not at all," I replied. "We might do that in time. What we are asking of you at this time is something entirely different. You have detained a shipload of passengers. You are to supply the ship with electricity and to provide food and water for the thousand passengers while the ship is detained here."

"The demands you are now making," replied M. Douain, "aren't in my province at all. I suggest, and request, that you do nothing drastic at this time which might confuse and harm our relations needlessly. We have no intention of using force. I shall look into your demands, and if you have no objection I shall visit the ship about five this afternoon. By then I may have some answers to your requests."

No, we had no objections, quite the contrary. We shook hands and parted. Then we headed for a nearby post office and put an urgent call through to Paris.

We told Ehud about our conversation with Douain.

"Very good," he said. "Keep applying pressure. Don't give up. We are busy here, in a quiet way, to get you out. Shaul and I have mobilized our best contacts and friends. Today they're meeting with Jules Moch, the Maritime Minister. Things look good. Be strong and keep your courage up. We are with you."

By the time we got to the *Ulua*, it was 4 P.M. The port was shrouded in semi-darkness. It had been snowing all day, and a thick mist blanketed city and sea. The policemen, wrapped in their snow-covered overcoats, patrolled the pier in pairs, trying hard to keep warm. The *Ulua* lay silent, wrapped in white. The frozen deck was deserted. Below, however, it was warm, too warm. The air was close with the warmth of hundreds of bodies, and the odors from the kitchen and toilets added to the oppressiveness.

But the passengers were not cheerless. Their appetites were perhaps somewhat dulled, the community singing was rather feeble, the men grew beards, but the morale was high. These young men and women had experienced the torments of hell; what was so bad about the warm belly of a good ship?

Inspector Douain arrived. Following the usual amenities, he asked to see the safety arrangements and rescue equipment, so that he could report to his superiors. Without any hesitation we took him below. M. Douain gazed in amazement at the hundreds of human beings stretched out in the bunks or moving about in the aisles. We showed him the fire-fighting stations, the life-belts and life preservers, the rafts and the boats.

The tour over, Inspector Douain said:

"At this point I still cannot tell you what is being decided about you. I shall report on what I have seen in the ship and then wait for a decision by the Ministry. At present I am authorized to tell you, in the name of the Le Havre Municipality, that in view of the condition of your passengers, and their being Jewish refugees, the Municipality has agreed to provide you, as of tomorrow, with sufficient food for as long as you remain in Le Havre."

M. Douain took his leave.

We did not know how to interpret his announcement. Could we now hope that somewhere the ice had been broken and the French were now going to deal more favorably with us, or was the contrary perhaps true and they were going to detain us, even at the cost of paying for our stay?

The next morning dawned gray and very cold, and our mood matched the weather perfectly. Again I went ashore and took a taxi to the shipping agent. No self-respecting shipping agent would be in his office at nine in the morning but I found a junior clerk there who recognized me and allowed me to phone Paris. Ehud came on the line. The decision, he said, would be made that morning. There was a chance that the Minister would issue an order to let us proceed.

The police were removed at four in the afternoon. Half an hour later the tugboats left us. Douain appeared at five, in high spirits. He shook hands all around, seated himself in the captain's cabin and told us how happy he was to have received the orders from the Ministry in Paris to allow us to sail. A cheer went up on the ship. The news traveled immediately to the dormitories below. I had an idea.

"Monsieur," I said to Douain, "I have a favor to ask of you. We have been in detention here for two days, through no fault of our own. We are not demanding to be indemnified, either by you or by the French Republic. We are glad that the incident is over. But you can compensate us with a small gesture on your part. We would appreciate it greatly if, in addition to the Swedish permit we already have, you would now provide a certificate from your office to the effect that we are allowed to carry a thousand passengers. After all, we are still on the first leg of our journey and may have to put in at another French port, where unforeseen difficulties may yet confront us."

We could see Douain debating with himself; man and official were locked in a duel. Then a little twinkle came into his eyes.

"Gentlemen," he said, rising, "prepare to weigh anchor. One of my officials will be here in an hour, and he will give you the reply to your request—which is not illogical." He shook hands warmly and left.

While Gad and his men made ready for departure, I hurried back to the agent's office and called Paris again. This time I got Shaul. I told him briefly about the change in our circumstances. I could almost hear the sigh of relief that welled up from his chest.

When I returned to the ship I found everything ready for sailing. As we waited for Douain's man, we allowed the passengers on deck for a breath of fresh air; they had been locked inside the ship for two whole days. About five hundred of them came up at one time and filled their lungs. The sailors aboard the adjacent Norwegian vessel gaped at the sight of the human wave surging up from the bowels of our small ship and swarming over her deck.

Douain's emissary finally arrived, bearing an impressive certificate on the official stationery of the French Maritime Ministry stating that, from the standpoint of safety and sanitary conditions, the good ship *Ulua* was authorized to transport up to a thousand passengers. We thanked the official and rewarded him moderately with good Danish aquavit, which Frenchmen like no less than Danes like French cognac.

We took aboard a pilot, weighed anchor and began moving out toward the open sea. The American Liberty ship turned its searchlight on us, and its crew was treated to the sight of a small ship laden with hundreds of people. We felt a great sense of relief. From all the decks a song rose softly in beautiful unison. The *Ulua* sliced serenely through the waters of Le Havre and turned its bow south to the Bay of Biscay.

Biscay

THE BAY of Biscay, toward which the *Ulua* was now sailing, was known to me from childhood days, not from my having ever sailed its waters but from Victor Hugo's *The Laughing Man* and the tale of the terrible storm which swallowed up the hero's ship.

I stood on the bridge that first night out of Le Havre and watched the black waves rising ominously and smashing against the ship's bow. "Ships' graveyard" is the name by which the Bay of Biscay was known to generations of sailors. I felt a queer sensation of cold and loneliness coming over me. I went down to the block where Tanya was sleeping. I was drawn to her. I wanted to see her face, enjoy her smile, touch her. The taste of that long kiss on the deck at night still lingered on my lips. Even during the Le Havre crisis I managed to see Tanya every spare moment I could, if only for an exchange of glances, a fleeting word, an eloquent touch of hands.

I approached her quietly, careful not to arouse those around her. I kissed her eyes lightly and whispered into her ear. She nodded her pretty head and slipped from the wooden bunk into my arms. I wrapped her in my heavy, warm greatcoat and carried her up to the forward deck. There among the anchor cables I spread out the blankets I had brought along and made a warm, sheltered nest for Tanya and myself. She curled up in my arms.

Tanya told me the story of her life—familiar, simple, terrible.

She was born in Kovno to a well-to-do family. Her father dealt in lumber. There were three children, all girls—Tanya, the eldest, Liuba, a year younger, and little Raya. Their childhood was pleasant and comfortable: many relatives, a good Hebrew school, playtime and holidays, vacations in the country, boundless parental love.

Then, like a sudden thunderstorm, came the Russians. Troops, armored cars, tanks overran the city. The family was torn apart. Some were banished to the depths of the Soviet Union. Those who remained in Kovno became wards of the Russians. Life was hard and tense, but not unbearable, until the Germans invaded Lithuania less than a year later and conquered it in a matter of hours. For Tanya, a young girl of sixteen, this was the beginning of a four-year nightmare. She was homeless, struggling against starvation, weakened by typhoid. Alone, her family wiped out, she was ultimately swept along by the tide of fate to the shores of Sweden.

I wanted to hear no more that night in the Bay of Biscay. I asked no questions. In the large pocket of my greatcoat, Tanya's delicate fingers squeezed mine. The wind and the night shrouded us in an eerie silence.

"Do you know the song 'Flowers'?" Tanya whispered softly.

"No," I admitted. "I know no song by that name."

"You mean they haven't taught you that song back home?"

I didn't think it wise to tell her the kind of songs we had learned in recent years around the campfires, such as "Shoshana, Shoshana, Shoshana, She Has a Wart on Her Eye."

"No, please sing it for me."

She looked up to see if I was making fun of her. Then she sang:

I shall go to pick flowers,
For flowers will heal my heart.
I am still so young,
I shall go to pick roses.

When I took Tanya back to her bunk it was almost dawn. I went up to my cabin and dropped down on my bunk. Until I finally fell asleep, a sailor's ditty kept going around and around in my head: "The Captain's in love, and how!"

From the depths of sleep, I could feel myself being tossed from side to side. I struggled to open my eyes. The cabin was in chaos—shoes, clothes, hangers, chairs, were swaying together, back and forth, in a bizarre dance. I staggered to the porthole, holding on to the walls to keep from falling. We were in a raging storm. Monstrous waves smashed against the ship. I managed to get some clothes on and made my way to the bridge. Gad was at the helm, worried, with Lopez, Art and Ephraim at his side. He pointed to the barometer. "This one's going to be a real storm," he said.

Uzi, Nissan and Miri arrived, and we all went to the command cabin. Gad pointed to our location on the chart. We were already in the Bay of Biscay. Should we try to get back to Le Havre? No, going back would be no less dangerous than going ahead.

The *Ulua* pushed through the heavy seas, thrusting her bow bravely into the storm. I went below. What I saw did not exactly fill my heart with gladness. Our passengers were clinging to their bunks, wrapped in blankets, their faces pale and drawn. Several of the sailors and a few of the hardier men kept going up and down the narrow aisles, passing out seasickness bags. Most of the people weren't even up to using the bags properly. They retched all around them, on the blankets and on each other. In that frightful congestion, none was left untouched. The kitchen was a garbage heap. Overturned tins of food, spilled sugar and the contents of broken bottles formed an oozy mass which was spreading everywhere, like the lava of a volcano. The air was close and acrid from one end of the hold to the other.

I went back on the bridge. The intensity of the storm mounted. I wanted to send a message to Paris to let headquarters know how we were doing and to inform them that we were continuing on our way south. Musik stayed on the transmitter and finally got through, but atmospheric conditions were such that reception was impossible. He finally gave up. "We're out of touch," he announced.

Nissan came up from below to announce that the bunks were splintering in the rough weather. We ran down. The danger was all too obvious. We recruited every man among the passengers who could stand on his feet, about two dozen. We summoned the Americans and the Spaniards. Here and there upper bunks had already plunged into those below, some of the passengers barely escaping. Scores of men and women wallowed in the abominable mess in the aisles, too sick and listless to move. We were deeply worried that the entire wooden structure might collapse beneath the weight of hundreds of people. We quickly distributed all the hammers we had, brought planks and began shoring up the weak spots. Cries of "This one's breaking" and "That post is cracking" kept the men dashing back and forth.

Up on the bridge Gad was battling the storm, maneuvering desperately to find a path in a sea gone berserk. At the wheel was Canadian Will, our most experienced helmsman. The *Ulua's* bow ripped through the water, dipping and rising, submerging and surfacing. Hundreds of tons of water smashed across her deck, sweeping away everything that was not securely tied down. From time to time the broadside impact of a mountainous wave threatened to capsize the vessel.

Gad, staring intently at the sea, shouted to me:

"Lucky we have a solid ship. The *Ulua's* an old warhorse. Any other ship, even a bigger one, and we'd be doomed."

"Can we get to some French or Spanish port?" I yelled.

"Right now I don't even know where we are," he shouted back. "It would be suicide to get too near the shore. We'd be thrown on the reefs and smashed to bits. We must keep going and ride it out."

The storm was now in its second day, and with luck should blow over in a day or two.

Musik came out of the radio shack, pale and haggard. "I couldn't get through to Paris, or our Marseilles branch, either. I did pick up a conversation between a Portuguese cruiser and the flagship of a British naval squadron. Both ships are not far away." We recalled that in Le Havre, we had heard a radio broadcast announcing that King George VI was leaving England on a state visit to South Africa. "You won't believe this," said Musik, "but the Portuguese is apologizing to the British squadron for its inability to salute His Majesty properly because of the heavy seas."

We found no solace in the king's misfortune. Uzi, scanning the seas with his binoculars, called out: "There they are, on the horizon!"

Through the glasses I could see the menacing silhouettes of the British battleships. I could make out an aircraft carrier, two or three cruisers and about six destroyers. They passed us at a distance of about four miles. They too were battling the storm, although they were travelling at twice our speed.

Ephraim came up from the engine room. We were being threatened with fresh disaster. Water was again seeping into the stern and contaminating our fuel. With the ship tossing as it was, a bucket brigade was out of the question. We could only hope that the fuel would not all be spoiled.

"The tanks!" Miri shouted, pointing forwards. "The covers are breaking!" Three large square metal tanks, each with a capacity of ten tons of oil, had been securely bolted to the deck. Now, battered by the waves and subjected to stress by the ship's rolling, the metal covers were beginning to crack. Oil spilled over the sides and soon a thick ooze crept along the deck, seeping through cracks in the deck and dripping into the hold. We tried to seal every crack, but the viscid black fluid penetrated the dormitories and soon an oily film clung to bunks, blankets, passengers. The filthy mess on the floor was churned into a morass in which everyone floundered.

But the worst was yet to come. The guy lines bracing the large tanks to the deck began to snap one after another. One of the tanks began sliding back and forth along the deck like a huge and angry robot. The wooden deck creaked and groaned beneath its every movement. Soon another tank tore loose. We were desperate. Unless we acted quickly, all three tanks would be sliding along the deck, destroying everything in their path. And what if the deck itself were to cave in under their ponderous blows? Unthinkable disaster would result. Swift action was needed.

Gad consulted quickly with Art and Uzi. In this storm it would be impossible to secure the tanks again. We had no choice but to jettison the tanks.

Several volunteer sailors armed with wrenches and hammers swarmed over the forward deck. They dodged past the tanks and opened a section of the ship's rails, then attacked the bolts and guy lines. Having loosened them, the men jumped back, at Gad's orders. The bow was now empty except for the three giant tanks, shifting back and forth like drunken Goliaths. Gad ordered the helmsman to heel the ship over to the right, a dangerous maneuver. Two of the tanks tore across the deck with a grinding noise, and plummeted into the sea in a frothy geyser, and disappeared into the ocean depths.

One tank was still on deck. Gad repeated the maneuver, but the tank refused to budge. Gad ordered the ship swung sharply to the right and then immediately to the left. This time the tank yielded and followed the others into the sea. We drew breaths of relief. It did not at all disturb us that we had lost all our fuel reserves which were to have brought us to our final destination. All we knew was that a disaster had been averted.

We were exhausted. The sea was still running high but we felt that the worst was over. Another stormy day passed. The waves were high, but no longer devastating. The sea dogs among us could already feel that the storm was abating; we could sense the calm that would follow.

Algiers

Along the Portuguese coast the sea was calm. We licked our wounds. The passengers were completely worn out. With some difficulty we found several dozen men still capable of standing on their feet, and they joined the sailors in swabbing the decks. The balmy winter sunlight and tranquil sea eased their toil. Only after we had cleaned the wooden planks of the layers of oil did we bring the people up on deck. They dragged themselves up the stairways and lay on deck completely exhausted, submitting to the sun's caressing rays and filling their lungs with the pure sea air.

Once the dormitories were vacated, work gangs of sailors and volunteers went below and plunged into the demanding task of cleaning the ship's interior and repairing the broken bunks. The kitchen was rehabilitated and provided buckets of tea for the people relaxing on deck. They still had no appetite for solid food.

Hours passed. The drawn faces slowly lost their tension. The passengers took heart. The girls began to do their laundry and strung lines to hang their clothes on. Gradually they lost their faded and woebegone look and regained some of their natural feminine charm. Their appetites improved and biscuits, soup and cheese had never tasted so good. Here and there on deck rose the sounds of singing and the strumming of guitars. Most of the people were reluctant to go below, preferring to remain on deck, wrapped in coats and blankets.

We took stock. Our reserve fuel tanks were gone. Some of the fuel in the remaining tanks was also ruined. Our fresh water system was damaged and its output reduced. We had to put in at a nearby port and take on fuel and water. A direct voyage to Eretz-Yisrael was out of the question. We discarded the original plan to rendezvous with a small wooden ship near Turkey, transfer the refugees, and then return to a European port for another cargo.

We sent a message to Paris. We had been out of contact throughout the storm, and headquarters had feared the worst, apprehensive that tragedy had overtaken us. Now we were informed that we would receive instructions in a day or two. Slowly we made our way to Gibraltar, intending to pass through the Straits at night to escape detection by the British.

The next day we were in the Mediterranean, having successfully negotiated the Straits of Gibraltar. Under the clear skies and a mild winter sun we were sailing east, east toward our goal.

That night, our first in the Mediterranean, was clear and beautiful. The stars played with their reflection in the water. On deck, Tanya rested in my arms—Tanya, for whose sweet lips I thirsted. I knew that this was my true love. Tanya needed me, too. I could be the haven with whom she could rest after the stormy years.

After a period of wretched suffering in the Kovno ghetto, Tanya was expelled to Latvia with her father, mother and two sisters. With thousands of other Jews they wandered in the Kaiserwald forest near Riga. Special SS units took them to Estonia. In a field screened by trees, the guns fired at the helpless Jews. Tanya witnessed the murder of all the members of her family. She fell to the ground and was spared, for the executioners did not stop to inspect their handiwork, but hurried away.

We were off Algiers, and no instructions had come yet from Paris. We contacted our Marseilles branch fruitlessly. Mossad headquarters was pondering the possibilities. We informed Marseilles that we had enough water and fuel for six days. If we sailed farther east, we would have passed the French ports, which were more or less friendly and where the certification we received in Le Havre could be useful.

We decided to put in at Algiers. We consulted the "Ports Register" for an Algerian shipping agent with a Jewish-sounding name, and a "Sami Cohen" appeared to answer our purpose. We approached Algiers and radioed Mr. Cohen, soliciting his help in laying in a supply of fuel, water and food.

From a distance Algiers looks like Haifa. While still out at sea, we had all the passengers go below, and we covered up all portholes. We were entering a Middle East city for the first time. Many of the people dealing with us here were bound to be Arabs.

We sailed into the harbor in the morning. The port was humming with traffic and the piers were crowded with people—Arabs in white burnooses, Frenchmen, uniformed soldiers, and, of course, Jews.

Sami Cohen was short, black of eye and hair, alert and smiling, with a good command of English. He came up on the bridge, bowed slightly and asked what we needed. I told him we needed fuel, water and food—vegetables, fruits and fresh bread. Casually, I said:

"Pardon me, Mr. Cohen. I understand you are a Jew?"

He hesitated a moment.

"Of course I'm a Jew." He was obviously not relishing what he expected to follow such a question. I said:

"Mr. Cohen, this ship is transporting a thousand Jews from Sweden to the Land of Israel."

The man stared at me with his coal-black eyes. His face went white as chalk, and he clutched the back of a chair. "*Shema Yisrael* (Hear, O Israel)," he said in a strangled voice. He gulped and recovered. "I know all about your sacred work," he said. "What a privilege to meet you face to face!"

I took Sami below. He wept as he followed me. He patted little Nurit on the head and kissed her, murmuring in Hebrew *akhenu b'nai Yisrael, akhenu b'nai Yisrael* (our brothers, the Children of Israel). We returned to the bridge.

"See here, sir," Sami said to me. "Your papers are in order. Nevertheless, I would suggest that you allow me to bring to you my good friend,Commandant Jacques Picot, an important port inspector here. He is not a Jew, but his relations with the Jews in Algiers, and especially with the Jewish shipping agents, are excellent. There is no risk at all in my telling him what I have seen on board. He will help you. He will also provide you with additional documents which you may need on your way east."

We agreed, and soon Sami Cohen brought Commandant Picot, a man in his sixties, short, with an aquiline nose and a trim gray beard. He wore a large Basque beret.

Jacques Picot went below and mingled with the refugees. He tried to talk with them in French, and then, meeting no success, he switched to halting German. He showed them a photograph of a blond boy with beautiful eyes.

"My only son," said the commandant. "He fell two years ago, fighting with the Maquis against the Nazis in defense of France. Like yourselves, I am a victim of the Nazis. I salute your courage."

The commandant sat there a long, long time, listening to the girls' stories. Then he returned to the captain's cabin, where he revived his drooping spirits with Danish aquavit. He affixed his own seal to the Le Havre document, certifying the *Ulua* for the balance of her voyage. We embraced Sami Cohen and bade Jacques Picot a cordial adieu. The ship was now stocked with all the fuel she needed. The larder was fully replenished with water, sacks of bread, baskets of fruits and vegetables. To be on the safe side, we asked Sami Cohen to give us the names of Jewish shipping agents and influential Jews in other North African ports.

The *Ulua* weighed anchor and sailed east, hugging the coast.

Philippeville

Musik was constantly at the radio which kept him in contact with Paris and Marseilles for instructions on our course, and with good reason, for in Marseilles Tami was at the transmitter. Morse code served Tami and Musik for their exchange of warm kisses and the wonderful words spoken by young couples. The official messages flashing between the *Ulua* and Marseilles were interspersed with love.

We had three alternatives. The first was to make directly for Eretz-Yisrael. This, however, would be inefficient and wasteful. A ship as large and as strong as ours should by our standards carry at least twice the fewer than thousand passengers we had aboard. Or we could adhere to our original plan and transfer the refugees to a small, hundred-ton wooden vessel somewhere between Cyprus and Turkey for the last leg of the voyage. This was now a highly doubtful possibility, however, fire having badly damaged the small ship we had planned to use. Our third course was to sail from North Africa to a port in France, Italy or Yugoslavia, take on several hundred more refugees and make for Eretz-Yisrael with a full cargo Paris debated the alternatives, and we cruised slowly along the North African coast.

Ephraim suggested that we take advantage of these days of waiting to repair the boilers and other equipment damaged in the storm. We studied our charts and located a small bay several miles west of the seaport town of Philippeville in eastern Algeria. There was apparently no village in the bay's immediate vicinity, which suited our purpose. When we approached, the bay seemed as quiet and desolate as we had expected. We anchored in the middle of the bay, and the engineers went to work. Ephraim said he needed two days for the repairs, and we decided to use the time for another no less important purpose—drilling the men aboard in rowing, rescue routines and especially personal combat tactics to fight off the British by whom we expected to be boarded. Such battle drill was already standard practice on our blockade-running ships. It consisted chiefly of hurling bolts and tin cans at the British sailors boarding the ship, hand-to-hand fighting with clubs and diving overboard.

Uzi, Miri and Nissan trained the hundred or so men we had aboard. Lifeboats were lowered, commands rang out. The men rowed round and round the *Ulua*. The deck resounded with the pounding of staves. The young men drilled with gusto. The women were barred from these drills, and they sat on the deck casually watching the men go through their paces.

It was a beautiful day. The sun warmed the deck and the passengers. The cove was well sheltered from the winds. The men shed their shirts, rolled up their trousers and plunged into the water. The deck began to look like a beach. The hundreds of young women stretched out to sunbathe, while others swam. Strangely enough, many of them had bathing suits or an improvised equivalent, some of them merely removing their dresses and sunning themselves in their underthings. The off-duty sailors gathered on the bridge and drank in the generous display of feminine beauty.

Our lookout called out that a vessel was speeding toward us from the direction of Philippeville, and soon a police launch drew up alongside. A young French officer saluted and asked to speak to the captain. He looked around with open amazement and curiosity.

"Certainly," said Art Bernstein. "I'm the captain. Come up on the bridge."

The officer politely declined. Would one of the ship's officers accompany him to the port administration to explain the ship's presence in the cove?

"Nothing to worry about," I whispered to Art. "Tell him I'll go along."

"Certainly," said Art to the officer, "our administrative officer will go with you."

Two officers received me courteously in the office at Philippeville Port. I showed them our papers, including the impressive document given me by M. Douain in Le Havre, reinforced with the seal of Commandant Picot of Algiers. The officers were satisfied. They thanked me for coming. It appeared that some nomad shepherds had come to them with a tale of a foreign warship on maneuvers in the deserted cove, and they had naturally sent a boat out to investigate.

We had put in for repairs, I said. As far as they were concerned, they replied, we could anchor there as long as we liked. Now that matters had reached this stage, would they consent to affix their seal to our certificate? *Certainement, pourquoi pas?*

I decided to take advantage of my visit to Philippeville. The officers recommended a merchant with a motor boat and a small barge who accompanied us to the local bazaar, where we loaded a cart with oranges, lemons, vegetables, fresh bread and other supplies. I paid cash in dollars, much to the delight of the vendors. From the bazaar we walked to the wharf, the cart rumbling behind us. On the way I asked the Arab merchant where I could find a silversmith. He guided me to a small shop, and I bought a thin silver bracelet with delicate arabesques. I had the silversmith engrave the date on the bracelet.

Relaxing on the laden barge, towed along by the chugging motor boat, I reached the *Ulua* toward evening. I could see the ship's lights in the distance. My heart was filled with warm emotion. The *Ulua* was my home. The people on board were my brothers and sisters. Their fate my fate. And there, too, was my beloved. Tanya, tonight I shall adorn your wrist with this bracelet. It will bind us together for many years. Many years.

The people aboard gave me a joyful welcome, as though I were bringing great booty. We held a conference. Ephraim announced that the *Ulua* would be ready to sail the next day. But where?

A message came from headquarters. We would receive a final decision in two or three days. This delay would again cost us considerable quantity of fuel. We decided to put in at the easternmost port of what was then French North Africa for fuel. Tunis was out of the question. The port was too large, and there were too many warships in the area. It would be better to put in at a small port. We selected Sousse.

I rose. My companions smiled. They knew whom I was impatient to meet.

I took Tanya's hand in mine and slipped the bracelet around her wrist.

"My Arthur," Tanya whispered, "what will become of us?"

"Arthur"—she didn't even know my real name.

"Whatever will be, Tanya, will be for us both."

I told her about myself, my family in Tel Aviv, my aged mother, my twin sister and older brother, waiting for me in a small house in the heart of the city. I told her something of my past. And Tanya resumed her own story. After the murder of her family she was caught and placed in a squad of Jews working at forced labor. For three years she wandered from one labor camp to another. In Stutthof she drove spikes into railroad ties. In bombed-out Hamburg, she worked in a munitions factory. Then she found herself in Bergen-Belsen with tens of thousands of other Jews, waiting for the end, for the freight cars which would take them to the crematoria.

One day she was ordered to join a group of girls chosen at random and was put on a train. Two days later they were transferred, freight cars and all, to a ferry. Next day, to their amazement, they found themselves in another country, another world. The car doors were flung open and the girls emerged to be welcomed by doctors, nurses, officers and ordinary civilians.

They had reached Malmo, in the south of Sweden. On the other side of the fence enclosing the area where the girls were to be taken through a complete clean-up procedure stood hundreds of tearful Jews from Malmo, waving to the bewildered girls.

The Jews of Malmo virtually adopted the girls, many families welcoming one or more into their homes. Tanya was taken into the home of "Pappi" Gordon, the cantor of the Malmo synagogue, a rotund and lovable old gentleman, a Lithuanian Jew who had known Tanya's family in bygone days. "Pappi" and "Mammi" had two sons at home—Willi, a sculptor, and Inge, a young engineer. Tanya was showered with love and affection, as though she were the couple's only daughter. Tanya was twenty, and her youth bloomed in this wonderful household.

A year passed. Tanya completed a nurses training course in a children's hospital maintained by nuns. But she felt that Malmo was not her home. Strong forces were drawing her elsewhere—to the Land of Israel. There she had an aged aunt and two cousins with whom she had been put in touch by the Red Cross, and many a tear-stained letter reached her from Eretz-Yisrael.

Tanya was drawn as though by a magnet to the pioneer youth movement founded in Sweden by the survivors of the European holocaust. With these youngsters she heard talk about the underground and blockade-running, duty and challenge, dedication and ideals. Here, after five years of repression, she experienced a revival of spirit.

That was how Tanya found her way to the Ulua*—and to me.*

Sousse

TWO DAYS later we reached the small and ancient port of Sousse in eastern Tunisia. Again the decks were cleared and the people swallowed up by the ship's interior. We sought out a Jewish agent from the list given us by Sami Cohen in Algiers. As soon as the port officials completed their official call on us, the agent appeared, accompanied, somewhat to our surprise, by an elderly man of dignified bearing, with a long beard, dressed in black and wearing a broad-brimmed hat. A rabbi, perhaps? Yes, it was the rabbi of the Jewish community of Sousse, the *Haham* David Bokovsa. We began to appreciate the efficiency of the "Jewish telegraph" in North Africa. From Algiers the news had gone forth to all the sea-port towns of North Africa:

"A Jewish refugee ship, the *Ulua*, is sailing along the coast in quest of aid and shelter."

Thus alerted, the Jewish community of Sousse was waiting. Now, while Gad dealt with the agent, I told the rabbi (he spoke beautiful Hebrew) something of our adventures. I took him below and showed him our *Sefer Torah*. He embraced it and fervently kissed its velvet mantle. I presented the religious youth groups to him. The rabbi blessed all of us, repeatedly. "From today on," he said as he parted from us, "I shall recite the Wayfarer's Prayer in your behalf every day until you reach the shores of our sacred land."

We remained in Sousse several hours. As we were casting off, at dusk, hundreds of Jews, men, women and children—young and old, but especially young—came running to the pier.

"Bon Voyage!" they shouted. "Shalom, brothers, shalom."

From the bridge and the decks we waved back, swallowing the lumps that rose in our throats.

Half a day out of Sousse, we received a message from headquarters in Paris:

"Proceed to Gallipoli in Italy. Be there day after tomorrow, 5 P.M. Alon's people will meet you. Refuel in Gallipoli. Sailing schedule to be determined with Alon. Same night pick up eight hundred passengers at Metaponte, then sail for Eretz-Yisrael. As of tomorrow morning your contact will be with Alon."

I summoned Gad, Uzi, Miri, Nissan and Ephraim and showed them the message. We were filled with excitement at this new development. The days ahead would be busy ones. Our first problem was how to accommodate eight hundred new passengers. The only feasible spots were the two storage areas in the lower hold at the stern. Both were full at the moment, one with drums of fuel and the other with the luggage our passengers had brought from Sweden.

Ephraim suggested that we empty the drums into the ship's tanks, since we would be refueling at Gallipoli in any case. As for the luggage, we had known from the outset that its chances of reaching Eretz-Yisrael were slim indeed. Early the next morning we went to work. Miri rounded up a score of robust men. Together with Ephraim's men and the engineers, they set about the grueling task of rolling the drums to the tanks, splitting them open with axes, emptying them into the tanks, and finally heaving them overboard. The gangs worked at a murderous pace. Stripped to their shorts, the men were soon covered with a clinging black film of oil which gave their bodies the gleam of burnished copper. As soon as the hold was empty we sent in a squad of men and women to swab it down thoroughly with brushes and rags, making it habitable.

While this work was under way, I called the passengers together on deck. They understood that something was up. I clambered up to a life raft and addressed them through a megaphone.

"Friends, tonight we shall have the privilege of taking on hundreds of other Jews bound for Eretz-Yisrael. We are now heading for Italy, where those brothers and sisters of ours are waiting for us.

"Our ship is strong and stout. No one knows this better than you. Together we weathered the storm in the Bay of Biscay. The ship can accommodate more people, twice as many as we have on board. We must take them on and accommodate them. Every square yard on the ship is precious. The new passengers will not have the luxurious appointments you have. In comparison, you will be traveling first class. But they must have some place where they can lay their heads. Our storage compartment is filled with your luggage. I know that all your possessions are in those valises. I also know how hard it was for you to gather your possessions and choose what you wanted to take along. Still, I want you to take out the items you need most, things which you cannot do without. Arrange these in bundles or bags and use them for pillows. The rest, and the valises, throw overboard. We shall ask for volunteers for hard work tonight, but first we must dispose of the valises."

An electric current seemed to envelop the people standing below me. Then came the voice of Ruhama, the leader of the religious girls:

"Fewer valises, more passengers! Girls, forward!"

Quickly, a double line was formed to the compartment. The long days on board ship and a common fate had welded the people into a single unit. I saw the girls taking sorrowful leave of each dress, blouse, pair of hose. But nothing dampened their spirits. One after another, valises, assorted garments, fuel drums, all were heaved over the side. The *Ulua* sailed on toward the tip of the Italian boot, leaving in her wake a long and colorful trail of empty fuel drums, suitcases, dresses, and frilly underwear.

At the mouth of the Gulf of Taranto we slowed down. We were to approach Gallipoli in darkness, to avoid needless attention. I stood on the bridge, thinking about the last time I was in Gallipoli, when Musik pointed to a light flashing from the port:

"They're replying to our call for a pilot," he said.

"Good."

"But their reply is in *Hebrew*," Musik exclaimed in excitement. I soothed him. During the past year following our adventure there a year earlier, our Italian Mossad people had turned Gallipoli into a base for repairing, refuelling and generally outfitting blockade-runners. I was not surprised, therefore, to receive signals from the port authorities in Hebrew.

Darkness was descending rapidly, and lights were appearing in the town.

"What are they sending?" I asked Musik.

"K-a-d-i-m-a-h ("Forward")!"

"Send back: S-h-a-l-o-m."

A fast boat came speeding to us from the port. We threw down a rope ladder. A moment later we were heartily embracing Leiser, Yisrolik and Danny. The Italian pilot with them seemed a bit forlorn among the *ebrei*. We sat with our "Italians" as the *Ulua* was being guided to the pier. They gave us details of our rendezvous, the location, zero hour, signal code with the shore, embarkation procedure and sailing time. They had brought us a good Italian meal and some Chianti wine, very welcome after the monotonous food aboard.

"Say," said Danny, "remember your Lucia?"

"Sure," I replied. "One doesn't forget the likes of her."

"Well," continued Danny, reaching for a glass of Chianti, "a toast to Lucia and her new husband!"

"Her new husband?"

"That's right," replied Danny. "Following your little escapade in Gallipoli, Lucia became a big wheel in town. Ada laid the groundwork, we came in and made Gallipoli our base of operations, and the sleepy little town suddenly grew quite prosperous. And who brought all this good fortune to Gallipoli? Why, Lucia, of course! Recently she married a police sergeant and is now a highly respectable matron."

I was really glad for her, and we raised our glasses:

"To Lucia."

We left Gallipoli at nine. No one went below to sleep. Tense and excited, everyone stayed on deck, standing at the rails. The girls leaned out, hair blowing in the wind and eyes straining into the darkness, as though they were expecting someone to appear out of the night and bring them tidings from the unknown.

Metaponte

A CLEAR, cold night. In the distance the lights of fishing villages twinkled faintly along the coast.

We were nearing our destination, the camp at Metaponte. I was familiar with this large embarkation center in the Gulf of Taranto from the days I had worked in Italy. Our code name for it was "Alaska." Strung out along the darkened beach at this very moment were hundreds of people, silent and tense. Knapsacks strapped to their backs, they were waiting for the small rubber dinghies which would take them to our ship.

The *Ulua* was barely moving. The seamen took soundings and called the figures to Gad. The shore line was an obscure mass.

We checked the time: 11.45 P.M. Musik flashed the signal, and from the shore came the proper reply.

We dropped anchor. Out of the darkness came the chugging of a motorboat, and we felt the gentle bump against the side. A ladder was lowered.

The first to clamber up was Ada—pretty, lively, flushed with excitement, as though this were her first such night operation. Behind her was the "Old Man" himself, Yehuda Arazi ("Alon"). There was no mistaking those lithe, tigerish movements.

Yehuda greeted us briefly, shook hands all around, then put an arm around my shoulders.

"The boys will soon be here in the first boat," he said. "Are you ready?"

"All ready," I replied.

Leiser gave the orders for the ladders to be lowered.

The first boat arrived; in it were several members of the Metaponte staff. They brought up one end of a heavy cable, which we made fast around the base of the anchor capstan. The other end of the cable was on the unseen shore. Along the length of this cable came the rubber boats, each with twenty passengers. The first contingent was already swinging up the ladders, helped by the sailors and our own men. A final swing, and over the rail they went on to the deck.

The operation proceeded quietly. Every newcomer was quickly taken below, out of the way of those following him. Guides stationed at the head of the stairway directed them to the storage compartments at the stern. The veteran "Swedes" lay in their bunks. Passengers with no duty to perform stayed in their places, so that the narrow aisles would be kept free. In the storage compartment, each arrival was shown the exact spot where he was to bed down. The guides were volunteers from the male "Swedes". The girls took no part in this action, but as the newcomers passed by their bunks they greeted them warmly: "Shalom"—"Shalom, friends"—"Shalom, friends."

Pale and drawn, the newcomers moved along the aisles, stooping under the weight of their knapsacks. They tried hard to smile back. Many murmured in awe: "An iron ship!" as they touched the metal bulkheads and pillars. These unfortunates were survivors from a miserable wooden vessel, the *Susanna,* which had tried to reach Eretz-Yisrael about a month earlier. When the vessel was wrecked, they were rescued and taken to Metaponte to wait for the next ship. The *Ulua* looked to them like a mighty vessel indeed compared with the frail craft that had almost become their coffin. Three out of every four were men, the usual ratio on blockade-runners, and they gaped with astonishment at the many women we had on board.

An hour passed. Three hundred of our new passengers were already aboard. As Ada, Yehuda and I were standing near the rope ladders, Uzi came running up from below: "Come on and see the sight of a lifetime!"

We hurried after him into the hold. Scores of people were crowded around one of the bunks, including a nurse with a first-aid kit. Sitting on the bunk, clinging to each other in a tight embrace, were two young women. One of our "Swedish" girls, lying in her bunk and watching the "Italians" file by on their way to the storage compartment, had recognized her own sister. They had had no word of each other since being separated by the war and taken to different concentration camps. Each had thought the other dead. Here in the hold of the *Ulua*, they found each other. After the first unbelieving cries of "Haya!" and "Sarah!", the "Italian" sister, Sarah, fainted in Haya's arms. Now she had recovered. We asked the crowd to move back and give the sister breathing space. A girl in a neighboring bunk immediately offered her place to Sarah, and the two sisters were reunited, exhausted but overjoyed.

It took three hours to get the eight hundred passengers aboard. The dormitories were jammed full. The *Ulua* was now carrying eighteen hundred men and women. Two Mossad men came aboard in the last boat. One was Yehezkiel, a farmer, short, broad-shouldered, smiling. This was our first meeting. His companion, I was delighted to see, was Avram, the man who had taken me out of the Santa Maria camp in his car about a year earlier. Avram, a member of an old *moshav* in the Plain of Sharon, was solidly built, persistent, courageous and reticent.

It was 3 A.M. Sailors, monitors, the Metaponte staff—all were staggering with fatigue. We comforted ourselves with the thought that in a few moments we would be casting off. But Ada had a surprise for us. She had gone ashore in one of the boats. Now she was aboard again. She held a whispered conference with Yehuda, and they approached me where I was standing with a group of my fellow sailors.

"Arthur," Yehuda began, "according to instructions from Paris the *Ulua* was to take on an additional eight hundred people here. This has been done, but Ada and I have a favor to ask of you."

Ada, always persuasive, took up the appeal.

"Out there on the beach is a group of about fifty boys and girls. You probably remember the orphanage in Salvino, up north, where we placed the hundreds of orphans we found among the refugees who came streaming into Italy. The youngsters on the beach are the oldest of them."

I thought I understood what Ada and Yehuda had in mind.

"It was decided to include them in Aliya Bet," continued Ada "We have the authority for it. They've been in Metaponte for two months. Every ship agrees to take them, but somchow they are always at the end of the line, after the adults. Each embarkation night we tell them: 'Children, we hope to put you on this ship.' They become broken-hearted all over again as the ship leaves without them. I don't have the heart to tell them that again there is no room for them on board. I know you are horribly crowded, but please take these fifty youngsters with you."

"Give us a minute to discuss it," I told her. But our conference was brief. I gave Ada a tired smile. "All right, Ada. How can we refuse you?"

Leiser took two boats ashore. I called in some of the American seamen and put it up to them.

"Gad and I will put half a dozen kids in our cabins," I said. "If it's all right with you, we'll ask you and our own men to vacate the crew's quarters and put thirty youngsters into your bunks. We'll take care of the others somehow. There are only a few days of travel left, and the nights are warm. Sleeping on deck shouldn't be too bad."

They agreed. Without comment, they emptied their quarters of all their personal belongings. Captain Lopez observed them and asked Gad what was happening. Why were the Americans and the others moving out? Gad told him about the children.

Not a muscle in Lopez's granite face moved as he listened. He then called over two Spanish sailors and spoke briefly to them. They nodded their heads and went off to move their gear.

The Salvino youngsters trooped aboard, hardly believing that the promise made to them was really being fulfilled. I took two girls and a boy to my cabin. Gad took two boys to his cabin on the bridge. All were asleep as soon as their young heads touched the pillows.

It was now 4 A.M. The weary ship was asleep. We gathered in the chart room for a cup of tea and a bottle of brandy.

"From here," said Yehuda, "you will sail directly to Crete. Up to that point you will stay in touch with me and come under my orders. Beyond that point, your contact will be with Eretz-Yisrael and that's where you'll get your instructions. I assume you will be told to make for a point on the southern coast, try to land the people and get out. According to our information, the British have expanded their radar screen and increased the number of destroyers and airplanes patrolling the coast of Eretz-Yisrael. Your chances of breaking the blockade are not too good. Because of your long route and many adventures, the British know more about you and your movements than about any other ship I can remember. If you do succeed in landing the immigrants, you will probably also be able to get away and come back to us here; if not, you'll get to Cyprus, in which case you'll be meeting many friends. Give them our regards."

We drank a toast: "To all our ships at sea!"

Ada, Yehuda, Leiser and the others of the Metaponte staff went ashore. The *Ulua* weighed anchor and set her course for the east: a pink strip on the horizon.

I went below, past the hundreds of sleeping people, to Tanya's bunk. I kissed her eyes, pressed my lips to hers, and whispered into her ear: "Good night, my love—and good morning."

I went up on the bridge. The children in my cabin were sleeping like little angels. I quietly took my sleeping bag and a few blankets and spread them on the deck, between the chart room and the radio shack. There I fell asleep.

On an Eastern Course

SAILING SOUTHEAST out of the Gulf of Taranto, the *Ulua* ran into a raging sea. The "Swedes," veterans that they were, rolled with the tossing of the ship, but the "Italians" were violently seasick. Their discomfort was further aggravated by the foul smell of the oil-soaked deck on which they had bedded down. The "Swedish" girls flocked to their aid, devoting themselves to the newcomers with extraordinary compassion. They found it pleasant to spoon-feed the strong "Italian" men in their moments of helplessness. The girls turned into practical nurses, served tea and lemon juice, cleaned them up when they retched and helped them up on deck for a breath of fresh air. It was easy to foresee that in the *Ulua*'s special circumstances, with hundreds of "Swedish" girls and hundreds of "Italian" men, romance would flourish.

On our second day in the Mediterranean, I called our men, who now included Avram and Yehezkiel, to the chart room for a conference to appraise our situation and examine the alternatives open to us. We had no rosy illusions about our chances of landing our passengers at one of the beaches and safely withdrawing. In fact, we still had no instructions as to where the landing should be attempted.

Most of the men, especially Uzi and Miri, were old hands at this kind of operation. Our main attention was focused on planning our resistance to the British Navy's ships if we were intercepted. We had accumulated quite a bit of experience. For the past six months, the British Navy had been intercepting blockade-runners and taking their passengers to detention camps in Cyprus. The orders from Mossad were to offer forcible resistance. This meant a battle with clubs, tin cans, bolts, fists.

All of us were prepared for this "war" between His Majesty's Royal Navy and the immigration fleet. It was imperative to convince the British that the Cyprus camps would not succeed, and that the

Jews would break through to Eretz-Yisrael no matter what the cost. This spirit animated the people of the Aliya Bet, Haganah and Palyam, but also, and perhaps most intensely, the immigrants themselves. They were struggling to raise themselves up from the dust and the ashes. After years of bowing to the lash of the whip, they sought to demonstrate to the world, and to themselves, that they had a cause worth fighting for and that they were prepared to return blow for blow. Now we made the *Ulua*, a one-time combat vessel, ready for battle again.

Back in Marseilles, Rudy and his men had devised an ingenious tactic designed to deceive the British destroyers and to deter them from approaching and boarding us with armed paratroopers. In one of the scrapyards in the port area, they picked up two wooden masts, thirty feet long. These masts were made fast to the deck of the *Ulua* amidships, one each port and starboard, lying parallel to the length of the ship. A spin of a pair of simple wheels, and these masts swung out at right angles to the ship, so that two long and threatening oars seemed to protrude from both sides of the *Ulua*. To camouflage the true nature of the protrusions, they were painted gunmetal color. To heighten the illusion, we capped them with balls of tar-coated cloth. These two wooden scarecrows were our "secret weapon."

From previous clashes with the British, we knew that the crucial moment came when they threw grappling irons aboard the blockade-runners so that their sailors and paratroopers could board them and seize quick control. We intended to delay this grappling maneuver as long as possible. Our fighting force consisted of about seven hundred fighting men—about a hundred "Swedes" and the rest "Italians." We divided this force into six units. a hundred men in the bow, a hundred and fifty amidships, a hundred and fifty at the stern, fifty on the bridge, fifty to defend the engine room, and a reserve unit of two hundred to be deployed in the hold in the stern from which reinforcements could be despatched to any sector as needed. Each unit was to be commanded by a Mossad man. It would be divided into sections and platoons, each consisting of men from the same pioneer training *(hachshara)* groups in which they had been organized before coming aboard. This would make for more efficient unit morale in combat. Each sector was to have its own arsenal of bolts, nails, tin cans, bottles and bits of scrap metal, strategically placed for easy access during the battle.

Special squads operating in support of the regular units would be provided with additional weapons. One platoon would repel boarders, engaging the paratroopers storming the deck in hand-to-hand combat, and would be armed with axe handles. Another platoon was to be equipped with fire-fighting axes to cut the rope ladders used by the British to grapple us together and thus prevent the paratrooper assault. The unit stationed amidships would be armed with two water hoses and an oil hose. The water hoses, used for swabbing down the deck, would direct jets of water against the attackers. The oil hose, connected to a special pump in the engine room, would spray them with hot oil—an invention of our own.

The command post would be on the bridge, where the ship's commander and his deputy would be stationed, with couriers to keep them in touch with unit commanders. Other couriers would maintain communications among the units themselves. Six first-aid stations, each staffed with nurses and medical orderlies, would be on duty on deck, while the ship's doctor and his staff would be in the sick bay to treat the more serious cases.

Our war council was over. We called in Art Bernstein and the American seamen and briefed them on our battle plans. As for our "armed forces," we still had four days at sea ahead of us, and these would be used for intensive training.

I went to look for Tanya. She was in the sick bay with a high-spirited group of nurses. My appearance was almost expected, as our relationship was no secret, although no one had any idea it was so deep and firm, it being assumed that this was a shipboard romance in which a ship's captain might indulge with an attractive passenger.

We made our way to the bow. Tanya and I had several favorite nooks among the coils of rope and the anchor chains. But the intimacy we could enjoy on the broad expanse of empty deck was shattered with the "Italian" occupation and the subsequent crowding. We finally found a spot where the congestion was not too bad, since anyone sitting here would have to endure a continous jet of cold spray. We fashioned a canopy out of my big windbreaker and nestled in its shelter. The world suddenly became warm and comfortable.

Tanya had no far-reaching plans for the future, other than living with her aged aunt and two cousins in Tel Aviv. She would have liked to be a nurse in one of the settlements, but now I had entered her life and she found herself in sweet confusion as though submitting to the new turn her life had taken—and to me.

"My dearest," I said, "we have only two or three more days aboard the *Ulua*. Then we may have to part. You and the others may reach Eretz-Yisrael and I may go back to Europe, or I may reach shore while you go to Cyprus. Everything is possible—the best and the worst. Tanya my love, if anything happens to me, if I am no longer alive, forget me quickly. But if I live, I will look for you. I have your address in Tel Aviv. Don't try to find me, you don't even know my real name. But that is not important. I am Arthur. You owe me nothing, Tanya, but I owe you all my love. If you agree, we shall make a home in Eretz-Yisrael, and you will be my wife and the mother of my children."

A shiver ran through Tanya's body and penetrated mine, like an electric charge. "Yes," she whispered.

Off Port Said

THE ULUA was sailing toward Port Said. The sea was calm, but the deck stormed with activity. The seven hundred men drilled diligently, lowering rafts and lifeboats in the hopeful event of an unobstructed landing and deploying in battle formations in the more probable event of a clash with the British. We received our first message from the special Haganah staff assigned to Aliya Bet in Eretz-Yisrael.

"Preparing for debarkation at Nitzanim beach seven miles north of Migdal. Will inform you later exact spot plus communication signals with shore. Debarkation to be handled by Palyam units, Palmach units covering. Estimated debarkation time three hours. Arrive midnight to enable return to open sea by dawn. Set course to reach point thirty miles off Port Said by noon, then change course and sail east full speed. At thirteen knots you will reach Nitzanim by midnight. Critical hours are between two and five P.M. in range of British scouting planes. If not discovered by nightfall, good chance for reaching shore."

We replied:

"Proceeding along international lane toward Port Said. Speed ten knots. Can quickly develop speed thirteen knots, even fourteen."

That same day, the second of our practice drills, Lopez, the Spanish captain, asked to speak to me privately. I led the way to my cabin and asked the children to leave us alone. I poured out some whiskey. The Captain sipped slowly, and the silence began to pall.

"Senor Arthur," he said finally, "you know very well how I got here. I've undergone quite a bit during my years at sea in war and peace. I'm an old sailor. I've learned not to let anything surprise me. When I was hired to sail with the *Ulua* I was told clearly, by you and the people in Marseilles, what it was all about. I'm not complaining. You haven't mistreated me or my men. We got our full pay before we sailed. Still, allow me to tell you that all that has been going on here, your drills and preparations—I must tell you that you are acting insanely." He paused to see the effect of his words on me.

"Captain Lopez," I returned, "I don't resent your words in the least. You have done your professional work well, and so have your men, the Spanish sailors. You have cooperated wonderfully and you've earned every penny you received. You shared with us equally in what little good we've had and in the great deal of trouble we've had. I am happy that you came to me to tell me your views. In any case, I have been meaning to talk to you about a change in your duty and the duty of your companions at the end of the trip."

The captain knitted his heavy brows. "Change in duty? What do you mean?"

I said:

"Captain, you have guessed right. We're likely to come up against British destroyers. They will try to board us and take us by force to concentration camps. We shall fight back with what little force we have. You and your comrades have nothing to do with this matter. That's our own concern. It's our battle. From the moment we are discovered by the British and clash with them you will be free of your sea duties. You will receive refugees' clothing and be given names of Jewish refugees. During the clash you will remain below with all the non-combatants. When you get to Cyprus, we'll find a way to get you out of there quickly and get you back to France."

The captain's face was pale. I watched a blue vein in his temple pulsate. He slowly drew his sailor's pipe out, filled it with tobacco and lit it.

"You don't understand me," he said. "I am not angry with you at all. You are a very young man and are responsible for the lives of hundreds of people. I'll try to make myself clear. When I said 'insane', I meant that you are taking a heavy risk and are casting all your people into it as well. All these drills in throwing bolts and cans, this waving of the clubs—all it will do is infuriate the British. They will shoot at you. Many victims may fall."

"We know all this, Captain."

Lopez shut his eyes, then opened them again.

"You said that this is your national struggle and that we have no part in it. You are right. We are for hire. We have tried to do our job thoroughly. But my friends and I have also come to feel for your passengers and to appreciate their spirit of sacrifice. I think they are fond of us, too."

"That's right, Captain."

"You interrupted me in the midst of my words," Lopez said. "What I wanted to say is that we Spaniards also have a feeling of pride and self-respect. If your decision is to follow this course, my friends and I shall follow it as well. We won't hide below with the women and the children and the aged. We'll be with you to the end, come what may."

"No, Captain, those are our standing instructions from above. It's an order."

The captain looked at me for a moment.

"Don't insult a Spaniard," he said quietly. "This would be an affront to which I could not submit. I cannot accept your order."

"Very well, Captain," I said. "We'll find a way of not disobeying orders and at the same time not hurting your feelings. I'll let you know."

"Thank you, Senor Arthur." Lopez rose and left the room.

I called Gad and Uzi and reported the conversation. We discussed the problem and decided that Gad would station the captain and the Spanish seamen below decks in the stern and in the engine room for auxiliary duty, but not on deck or on the bridge.

Port Said was still two days away. Gad charted our course carefully and kept us at a speed calculated to put us at a point north of the entrance to the Suez Canal, from which we would change course for El Arish at the exact hour we wanted, between ten and eleven before noon. We gave headquarters our exact course, and received further instructions as to the debarkation point, the signals, landing procedures, how to handle possible clashes in the course of the landing, and retreat routes.

Another day passed. We halted the drills to give the men some rest before the final, decisive stage. The light-heartedness which marked the first three days of drill now vanished. The men sat about in small groups, quiet and withdrawn. Now we were given our Hebrew name, to be used in case of capture. Our usual procedure was that a ship eluding capture remained anonymous and returned to a European port to continue its work under its foreign name. If captured, as most were now destined to be, her name was immediately changed to a symbolic Hebrew one.

We were now the *Haganah Ship Haim Arlosoroff,* named for a brilliant young leader of the Jewish community in Eretz-Yisrael who had flashed comet-like across our skies and fallen at the height of a lustrous political and public career. The men took the large blackboards we had bought in Marseilles and painted on them, in large white Hebrew and English letters, HAGANAH SHIP HAIM ARLOSOROFF. We also produced two large blue-white flags, the flag that was eventually to become the flag of the State of Israel. We placed one at the base of the high mast on the bridge and one near the flagpole in the stern.

We were ready for battle.

Towards Nitzanim

AT DAWN on February 27, we brought our passengers on deck for a last breath of fresh air before the operation. The *Ulua* sliced through the water. Our immigrants ate their breakfast in silence. Soon we would reach the point beyond which no one was to show himself. All would be secluded in the bowels of the ship.

We gave headquarters our position, and at 10 A.M. imposed radio silence. Gad steered the *Ulua* on an eastern course. The passengers went below and took up the positions assigned to them. Except for a few sailors on duty the decks were empty. Nothing showed on the horizon. We sailed east at full steam. Every minute was precious.

We had a quick snack for lunch, standing at the rail on the bridge. Gad transmitted brief instructions to the helmsman. At 1 P.M. we were within range of the British patrol planes. The *Ulua* approached its full speed, twelve knots, thirteen knots, coming up to fourteen—the maximum. The little ship trembled as she cut a swath of foam in the calm sea. Three more hours passed. We were somewhere between the Bardawil Marshes and El Arish, still a good distance from shore. Another hour and twilight would come on; in two hours darkness would spread its canopy over us. We might yet succeed in eluding the planes and reach Nitzanim safely.

A few minutes before five Gad called out:

"There it is!"

A small black speck in the sky, growing larger. Another minute, and we could hear its motor—a Halifax bomber. At first it circled above us at a high altitude, then swooped down like a hawk, almost grazing the mainmast. I said to Musik: "Try opening the receiver, he may be sending." Musik twirled the dials and immediately heard the pilot's transmission. He was talking with the British Naval Base headquarters at Stella Maris on Mount Carmel in Haifa.

Halifax to Stella Maris: "My position 31.33 north, 33.05 east.

I am circling over a vessel that looks like a naval vessel, sailing from the direction of Port Said toward El Arish."

Stella Maris to Halifax: "Describe the ship. Describe the ship."

Halifax to Stella Maris: "Ship looks like small corvette or minesweeper. No cannon visible. Strange superstructure at stern. One stack painted dark gray. Cannot make out name or flag."

Stella Maris to Halifax: "What is ship's speed? Are there many people on deck?"

Halifax to Stella Maris: "I estimate her speed at twelve knots. Not many on decks. I see three or four in the stern and two or three on the bridge."

Stella Maris to Halifax: "Don't let ship get away. Keep circling above her. Ship is *Ulua*, at sea for a month on way from Sweden to Palestine. In hold are about two thousand Jewish illegal immigrants, organized by Haganah. We are sending destroyer D-15, now near Gaza, to intercept her. Until destroyer gets there, maintain constant visual contact with *Ulua*."

For a moment we considered turning tail and running. In the darkness we might elude the plane and the destroyer, but we knew we had no chance. The destroyer was twice as fast as we were. We continued full speed ahead to our rendezvous.

It was still daylight when we spied the destroyer. It came from the north. The last rays of the setting sun glinted on its long silhouette, which appeared larger by the minute. Now it came to within a few hundred yards of us, swung about in an arc and continued in the same direction, parallel to us.

As darkness set in a second destroyer joined the operation, also first circling us and then attaching itself to the escort. We broke our radio silence and informed headquarters in Eretz-Yisrael that we were trapped. We asked for instructions as to where to land the ship and the passengers, using force.

One of the destroyers drew near and began signalling with its large searchlight:

"What is your name?"

"*Ulua,*" we replied with our own signal lamp.

"Your flag?"

"Honduras."

"Where from?"

"Port Said."

"Where bound?"

"Alexandretta."

"What are you carrying?"

"We have fifteen hundred shipwreck survivors picked up after a storm."

The destroyer halted its interrogation.

Our headquarters informed us that plans were being discussed to get thousands of Tel Avivians to the beach at midnight, when we should be opposite the city. We would head for shore and try to run on a reef. Scores of small boats of such organizations as "Zebulon," "Hapoel" and Sea Sports Clubs, as well as private craft, would go out and pick up the refugees. Were we prepared for such a plan?

We were.

Nine o'clock. Two other destroyers joined our escort. We were in true battle formation surrounded by the enemy. The destroyers played their powerful searchlights on the *Ulua,* gradually approaching us in the light of their beams. Then they executed a more complicated maneuver. They approached us in pairs and criss-crossed us with their lights. Finally they all closed and caught us in their mighty shafts of light. The beams blinded us and made navigation difficult. White with anger, Gad went to the signal light.

"We are not in territorial waters. You are violating international law and are interfering with our course. Let us alone."

No reply.

We brought the *Ulua* to a stop. The destroyers stopped.

Gad repeated his message and we moved off. The destroyers remained where they were. We sailed on. That entire night the destroyers followed in our wake, keeping us within searchlight distance, but they no longer played games with us.

About 10 P.M. we were told by headquarters that debarkation at Tel Aviv at midnight would be too dangerous. We would in all likelihood lose many people in the darkness and confusion and would suffer many casualties. We were to continue to Haifa and try to land there in broad daylight.

We went below and told the people of the new developments. Tomorrow would bring on the battle. Tomorrow the issue would be decided. Now let the combatants sleep and gain strength.

Pursuit

DAWN. THE first streamer of light in the east. We were sailing north in international waters, about five miles offshore. Daylight revealed the four destroyers escorting us, two on each side. Their decks were quiet, their men asleep. To the east rose the southern cliffs of Mount Carmel. We allowed the passengers to come up on deck and glimpse the Land of Israel from afar, first in small groups, then by the hundreds. Within half an hour everyone was on the starboard side, facing the shore, and the *Ulua* listed heavily. I had to caution them time and again against crowding on one side all at the same time. The sun rose slowly from behind the Carmel range. Ruhama's girls broke into song: *Between the borders in the trackless hills.* Soon from hundreds of throats came the thunderous words: *For him, also, who shut tight the gates, will come a day of revenge and reckoning.* The decks of the destroyers came to life. Their sailors, aroused by the singing, stood by and listened silently.

We began to bring up our ammunition. In the stern, amidships, in the bow, heaps of hardware took shape—bolt, cans, kitchenware, nails, hooks, spare parts, scrap metal. There was also visible activity on the decks of the two destroyers nearest to us. We could see, even without the aid of glasses, squads of sailors in blue-gray battle dress, steel-helmeted and armed with staves, shields and side arms.

At seven we passed Atlit. From a distance we saw the lofty Crusader tower protruding from the shore. We were careful to keep outside territorial waters.

At 7.15 two submarine chasers came speeding toward us from the direction of Haifa. These were smaller than the destroyers and sat lower in the water. They deliberately came very close to enable us to see for ourselves that they were filled with armed commandos equipped with rope netting.

The submarine chasers churned up the water around us, then

veered sharply to the north and joined the destroyer escort. We were now proceeding in a hexagon, the *Ulua* in the center, the two pursuit boats in front, a destroyer on either side, and two more bringing up the rear.

We saw Stella Maris at the western tip of Mount Carmel, the naval headquarters from which the struggle against us was being directed. At 7.40 A.M. Gad began moving the *Ulua* close to the three-mile limit. The six escort raft followed suit, maintaining their formation. At 8.20, some distance away from the mouth of Haifa Bay, we drew close to the three-mile limit. The destroyer to our east, between us and the shore, was apparently the enemy flagship. It now made a sharp turn and drew almost a ship's length away. From the bridge of the destroyer, which towered several yards above us, a loudspeaker blared:

"Jewish refugees, you are now entering the territorial waters of Palestine. Under the regulations of the Mandatory Government, you are breaking the law and are entering the borders of Palestine illegally. I am instructed to extend you this warning. His Majesty's ships stand ready to direct and escort your ship to the island of Cyprus. There you will be landed and accommodated in camps, in comfortable circumstances, and remain there temporarily until your fate is decided."

All the refugees were on deck. They stood massed together, pale, tense. We of the crew—our own men, Americans and Spaniards—were crowded among them, dressed like them. From our deck a voice replied in English:

"Sailors of the British Navy, before you is a ship of Jewish refugees who are returning to their homeland after a long exile and after the murder of their people by Hitler and the Nazis. It is not we but you who are violating humanity's law by detaining us. It is not we but you who are in this country illegally. The Land is ours and ours she will continue to be. Our brothers are standing on shore waiting for us. No one will stop us. We shall resist you—and win."

The British destroyers closed in on us. The voice from the flagship continued:

"When you cross the three-mile limit, we shall fire a warning shot. If you do not stop, we shall have to use force."

The two signs bearing our Hebrew name, *Haim Arlosoroff,* were raised simultaneously on both sides of the bridge, in plain view of the British. I raised the megaphone to my lips:

"Brothers and sisters, in a few minutes we shall be within the borders of our Land. You all know your duty. If we are courageous, this land will be ours. No power, not even the one now confronting us, will take it from us. Let us sing *Hatikva."*

The first strains of *Hatikva* ("The Hope") rolled over the ship like a huge wave. The flag—our blue-white flag with the Shield of David—was unfurled at the top of the mainmast, and another was raised in the stern. The hour was 8.58. Musik, now in constant touch with headquarters, radioed them:

"We're going in!"

The destroyer again drew near, this time to a distance of about twenty yards. The loudspeaker:

"We want to talk to the captain of your chip."

No reply.

"Captain, you are taking responsibility for the lives of many hundreds of men, women and children on the decks of your ship. We shall use force against you if you go in. Captain, identify yourself."

No reply.

"Who is responsible for the ship? Who is the captain who has taken your fate in his hands?"

There was a ten-year-old boy aboard, Lova, who had joined us in Italy, a lovable mischievous redhead. I saw him standing nearby. I ran to my room and returned with my gold-braided officer's cap. I called Lova and crowned the youngster with the cap, which came down around his ears and over his forehead. We handed him a large pair of binoculars and told him to go up to the lookout point on the bridge. He climbed up the stairway and stood there, alone, smiling, in full view of everyone. Someone on our deck called out:

"Look, this is our captain! For his sake and in his name we're going to fight you."

The destroyer drew off until it was about a hundred yards away, then fired a warning cannon shot across our bow. We ordered all non-combatants below. On deck stood the seven hundred men trained for resistance.

The Battle

Two of the destroyers increased their speed and headed straight toward us. The hour was 9.05. Musik cabled to headquarters:

"The battle is beginning."

Aboard the *Ulua* an order was given and the ship quickly swung out the two scarecrow oars, one on each side. The surprise was complete. The destroyers slowed down; instead of trying to come alongside, they approached us astern. One of them rammed our stern with its steel bow. The *Ulua* took the blow and skidded to one side. At that moment a dense cloud of steel bolts and tin cans rose from the deck and came raining down on the destroyer. The British sailors protected themselves with the shields they were holding and sought cover behind the rails. Several of them were hit. The second destroyer now came in at the stern, and again the *Ulua* shivered under the blow. We rained another iron barrage on the enemy.

9.12 A.M. Musik radioed:

"First attack repulsed."

The two destroyers came at us again, one on each side. Two jetstreams of water shot out from them at the men in our stern and sent them sprawling, but they sprang to their feet and hurled their makeshift ammunition with renewed wrath. One of the destroyers almost touched us, and two jets of water shot out from the *Ulua*. At that close range they were able to knock several British sailors off their feet and drench a good many more.

A message from headquarters:

"Be strong. Have courage!"

We were now in Haifa Bay. We intended to burst through as closely as possible to the ships moored at the big breakwater in the port. Half a dozen freighters were anchored there, waiting for citrus cargoes. If we could reach them the British ships would be unable to maneuver and ram us, and our people would be able to go overboard.

The British apparently divined our purpose. By ramming the *Ulua* repeatedly, they forced her to head for Ras el-Krum and Bat Galim. The *Ulua* proved to be highly maneuverable. Many times we avoided ramming by swinging the helm about sharply at the very last moment, causing the destroyer to miss its mark. Our men on deck had to cling tightly to solid support as they swayed wildly in the wheeling ship. But the battering went on. One of the destroyers collided head-on with the *Ulua*, bow to bow, badly damaging us. Somehow, instead of capsizing, the *Ulua* righted herself, but an ugly hole gaped in her bows.

Despite everything, the *Ulua* sailed on, but it was clear that the incessant ramming had sufficiently disabled us so that we could not reach port. We did get in close to shore, but not at the desired point. Our showers of bolts and streams of water—perhaps, most of all, our "guns"—had so far prevented the destroyers from grappling us and sending a boarding party over our side. It was a draw.

But here one of the destroyers took the risk. Moving swiftly, it came alongside, its side grating against ours. We did all we could, hurled hundreds of bolts and cans, sprayed water and hot oil, but in vain. The destroyer's bow snapped our gun-barrel mast like a matchstick, at the same time crushing the lifeboat swinging from the side.

Our secret weapon was no more. The British went for the second mast and smashed it as easily. The *Ulua* remained bare and exposed. Now came the submarine chasers with their commandos and nets. From one of them a large rope-net edged with grappling hooks came flying and caught on our stern, clinging like a leech. Several commandos were already climbing up hand over hand. The commander of the unit in our stern gave the word and the axe-wielders sprang forward and hacked at the ropes. The net fell back on the commandos thrashing about in the water. They were fished out by their comrades.

10.12. Musik radioed: "They are trying to board, but are thrown back."

We could see the houses of Bat Galim strung along the beach. Gad maneuvered desperately in an attempt to push into the bay, but the destroyers kept nudging us to the Bat Galim "Peninsula," where there was a large British army camp. The camp was now occupied by units of the Sixth Division paratroopers, the famous "Anemones," so named for their brilliant red berets.

The submarine chasers again attacked the *Ulua*. One hurled two nets at us and the other came close enough to enable the commandos to board us. Our axe-men cut down one net, and we shook the second off by a sharp veering maneuver. About a dozen British soldiers advanced along the *Ulua* deck. We had an auxiliary unit of a hundred men in the stern, some armed with clubs, under the command of Nissan and Yehezkiel. For a moment, all was confusion, then suddenly we saw our men writhing on the deck. The advancing commando unit seemed to cut them down as though with a scythe. Uzi ran toward the scene and returned immediately to the bridge to report.

"Gas!"

The commandos had cylinders of tear gas strapped to their backs and were holding hoses whose nozzles they aimed at our men, blinding them and forcing them to retreat. This unit could take over the entire ship! The reserves! The reserves! We had to bring in the reserves! Uzi raced to the reserve unit under Miri's command. He quickly led about fifty men through one of the hatches in the stern. They emerged behind the British commandos, who were advancing in a line of battle extending the width of the ship, spraying tear gas, unaware of the danger behind them.

Our men attacked the British with their clubs. Some of the commandos tried to turn around and aim the tear gas at their attackers, but they were struck down and their tanks smashed. Two were seriously wounded, and their blood trickled along the deck. Some of our men were also bleeding, and scores lay where they had fallen. The British raised their hands and surrendered. In the heat of battle our men hurled two of the commandos overboard. I ran up to put a stop to this, and ordered that the soldiers who surrendered were to be treated as prisoners of war. Their wounded were to be taken to the sick bay along with ours.

10.15. Musik radioed: "Several soldiers have boarded us. They are spraying gas. Two were thrown into the water, the others surrendered. Their weapons were thrown overboard."

An urgent message from headquarters:

"Don't endanger people's lives!"

We replied:

"Their wounded are being treated."

All this time we were being nudged steadily toward Bat Galim. We could clearly see the swimming pool and the artillery camp where I had served several years earlier. The beach was lined with hundreds of British paratroopers, jeeps, Bren-gun carriers, all forming a large and threatening semicircle. We also saw a stream of demonstrators, carrying placards and flags, converging on Bat Galim.

The destroyers rammed us with increasing viciousness. The results of the first clash had evidently enraged them. A few hundred yards from the beach the British made a mighty last effort to subdue us. Two destroyers cut into the path of the *Ulua* to force her to a stop, while the submarine chasers ranged alongside with their nets. The commandos began to climb the netting, many of them becoming entangled in the ropes. A battle raged at the rails. A few commandos were thrown overboard, but about fifty succeeded in boarding the ship. What happened next was what we had most feared. The British opened fire.

Joe, his stomach riddled with bullets, fell from his perch in the crow's nest, where he had been stationed since the beginning of the battle. He landed at our feet on the bridge. Joe, the redheaded ex-Marine, veteran of the fighting in the Pacific. The British had seen him in the crow's nest and evidently thought that he was directing the action, and they shot him down.

The battle of clubs against gas still raged on deck. In the stern, where the strongest British force was concentrated, our fighters' resistance was weakening. Amidships, our men fought grimly. Wounded from both sides lay on the deck. Avram, who was directing the battle, had taken a heavy blow on the head, and his face was streaked with blood.

The commandos' objective was our bridge. They wanted to take the ship "alive" and sail her into port. Our proper course of action suddenly became clear. We must beach the *Ulua*, sail her on a reef in full view of Haifa and the entire community. Gad sent the ship plunging ahead.

"Two hundred more yards and we'll be in shallow waters," he yelled to me. "The chasers won't be able to follow us. We have to hold out, we can't let the commandos capture the bridge or the engine-room." These were clearly the enemy's objectives.

10.26. Musik radioed:

"We are landing in ten minutes."

In the meantime the commandos had gained control amidships. They split into three columns. One advanced to the bow, where it came up against strong resistance on the part of our last fighting unit. Another column stormed the stairway leading to the bridge. Step by step the British fought their way up, advancing steadily. A third column broke open the windows of the engine-room and threw in tear-gas bombs.

The *Ulua* was now sailing toward Bat Galim by herself. The destroyers and submarine chasers did not dare to follow us into the shallow water, with its dangerous reefs. Only a hundred yards separated us from shore. A few more minutes and the battle would be over. Uzi and Nissan stood in the bow, ready to order a group of some twenty men to dive overboard and swim to shore.

"Jump!" Over they went. They had not the ghost of a chance of escaping the hundreds of paratroopers lining the beach, but never would it be said that none of the *Ulua* immigrants had succeeded in breaking through and treading the soil of the Land of Israel.

A squad of commandos led by a blood-stained second lieutenant was fighting their way toward us. On the bridge were Gad, the helmsman and I. Between them and us were twenty immigrants, and they fought like lions. I glanced at the beach: fifty yards.

10.29. Musik radioed:

"About to land."

I ordered Musik to break off contact. A few more minutes and the British would be in possession of the transmitter. At 10.30, he radioed his final signal. Headquarters acknowledged with one word: "Courage." Musik pressed a button and detonated a number of explosive charges that had been placed in the apparatus that served us so well these long months. It would not fall into the hands of the British intact.

Gad issued his last two orders. Into the speaking-tube, to Ephraim in the engine-room, he called out: "Open the scuttle valves!" Then, to the men in the bow, which the British had not yet taken, he shouted: "Drop both anchors."

In the engine-room, now full of tear gas, Ephraim and his men worked at the boilers like madmen to give the *Ulua* a final spurt of speed to cover the last few yards to shore. Ephraim ordered the men to open up the valves embedded in the deck, so that the water flooding the *Ulua* would settle her on the reefs. The sailors began to open the big valves just as the commandos, having overcome the last of the defenders, came bounding down the stairway to the engine-room. They saw what was happening and leaped forward to close the valves, but it was too late. A mighty flood of water surged into the engine-room, and seconds later the British had to flee along with our men. Slowly the ship began to settle. The anchors dropped with a thunderous roar of their heavy chains, and bit in among the reefs. The *Ulua* sank, shuddering violently as she settled on the reefs about fifty yards offshore.

The infuriated commandos charged the bow, shooting as they came, in an effort to reach the anchors. The wounded officer and his men gained the bridge, waving pistols.

"Hold your fire," I shouted to him in English.

"Order your men to stop fighting," he shouted back.

"Stop fighting," I yelled to the men in the bow.

"Cease fire," the officer ordered his men.

We took advantage of the moment it took him to give the order to his men and jumped down from the bridge to mingle with the hundreds of men on deck. The young officer suddenly realized that he had allowed the ship's commander to slip away. He recovered quickly and yelled down to the commandos below:

"Go after the men who jumped from the bridge! Hold them!"

But his words were lost in the tumult. There were some shouts of "Which ones?" "Where'd they go?" and that was all.

An eerie silence suddenly descended on the ship. No sound was heard other than the groans of the wounded. Theirs and ours were being given first-aid by the nurses and medical orderlies. The hundreds of immigrants sat down listlessly wherever they happened to be, defeated, bruised, their eyes still tearing, soaked to the skin, wet, dirty, their clothes in tatters. Those who had dived into the water were fished out and led away. Almost within arm's reach were the trim white houses of Bat Galim. Behind the barrier created by a wall of British paratroopers, hundreds of demonstrators waved their hands and shouted unintelligible encouragement.

The commandos took up positions on the *Ulua*. A command unit was posted on the bridge and others were stationed fore and aft, submachine-guns at the ready and pistols drawn. Fast motor launches brought police and army officers, plainclothesmen, and army doctors. They made a quick inspection of the ship. The seriously wounded commandos and immigrants were lowered on stretchers to a launch which sped away to the port.

It was obvious that the British were in a dilemma. The *Ulua* now stuck in their throat, so to speak. They held a lengthy consultation and apparently decided to drag the ship off the reef on which she was resting and tow her to Haifa Port. A call was sent out for the two tugboats in port. First the British tried to raise the anchors. This had to be done manually, since our engine-room was now dead. But scores of our men clung desperately to the anchor chains and refused to budge until forcibly removed by the soldiers. For an hour the British then toiled, the sweat pouring down their faces, attempting to raise the heavy anchors, but to no avail. The flukes had lodged deep among the reefs and could not be moved an inch. The British sailors cursed the anchors, the reefs, the bloody ship and the refugees.

One of the tugboats attached a heavy steel cable to our bow. The tugboat groaned and grunted. Thick smoke poured from its funnel. The *Ulua* shivered—and the cable snapped. Both tugboats now attached cables. Again a mighty effort. The tugboats strained. Both cables snapped.

It was very quiet aboard the *Ulua*.

Noon. The people sprawled about on deck, exhausted, suffering, waiting. Shortly before two o'clock the first group of landing craft arrived and were moored to the ship. The British commander on our bridge raised his megaphone:

"Jewish refugees, we are going to transfer you to the landing craft and then to ships which will take you to Cyprus. Aboard these ships you will be given hot meals. In Cyprus you will be placed in detention camps, under good conditions, until His Majesty's Government decides what is to be done with you." A British sergeant translated the words into Hebrew.

Silence on deck.

Scores of paratroopers clambered up from the landing craft and joined the British commandos, sailors and police on our decks. The commander again raised his megaphone: "Get up and start moving to the landing craft. Our soldiers will help you."

No one stirred. As in obedience to an unspoken command, the hundreds of refugees lay down on the deck. Not one remained sitting or standing up.

In squads of four the soldiers advanced on the people lying closest to the landing craft, seized them by their hands and feet and dragged them away, kicking and struggling. The men and women bit and scratched the hands of the soldiers. The British showered blows on them and twisted their arms painfully. The boats filled up, about a hundred refugees in each, and made for the port, each carrying a guard of paratroops armed with submachine-guns. The crew of the *Ulua* was taken along with the others, but we tried to have some of our men on each of the boats.

I was battling the four soldiers who had seized me when I saw Tanya being led away by several paratroopers to one of the boats. During the fighting, she was stationed at a first-aid station amidships. She was still wearing the Red Shield of David armband. Her white smock was torn and stained with blood and iodine. Tears rolled down her cheeks. She disappeared into one of the boats. I was taken to another.

The barges approached Haifa harbor, which had been completely sealed off by the British. One after another the boats were moored to a pier among the destroyers. There were many freighters in Haifa port, flying flags from all over the world, and their crews lined the rails to stare at the drama. The area was filled with hundreds of British soldiers. We were forcibly dragged from the barges and pushed into a long line leading to one of the warehouses.

Inside, we were set upon by a squad of British and Arab orderlies armed with huge DDT spray guns. One by one we were pushed into a shower of white disinfectant. When we emerged, our faces were caked with a porridge of sweat, grime, traces of tear gas, crusted salt from the sea water and DDT. Our clothes were in tatters, our shoes soaked in mud and oil. Most of the people had somehow managed to retain their knapsacks on their shoulders. Some, however, were taken to Cyprus with nothing but the rags they wore on their exhausted bodies.

We were led to the other end of the pier, where deportation ships were waiting. I noted the name of the ship into which we were being loaded: *Empire Rival*. She was outfitted expressly for deporting "illegal" immigrants. The dormitories were enclosed by heavy steel netting. The portholes were barred. We were pushed into a large dormitory where hundreds of mattresses and army blankets were laid out in rows. Completely exhausted, the refugees slumped to the mattresses, some falling asleep at once. A few lined up at the faucets set into the walls in the corners, washed their burning faces and rinsed their mouths. Hours passed. The ship filled up with hundreds of refugees. The doors were slammed shut.

Soldiers appeared with buckets of tea and porridge. Some of our men rose up, seized the buckets and flung their contents on the deck and at the soldiers. A sharp scuffle broke out. The soldiers left and locked the doors behind them.

Evening fell. Through the portholes we could see Haifa and Mount Carmel, twinkling with thousands of lights. Giant searchlights on the pier and on the destroyers played their beams on the *Empire Rival,* on the lookout for Palyam frogmen. During the night the *Empire Rival* weighed anchor and sailed for Cyprus. I made my way among the refugees, trying to comfort them. I could not find Tanya. I assumed she was aboard one of the other deportation vessels.

The *Ulua*, too, was wrapped in darkness.

When the last of the refugees was removed, squads of British soldiers and sailors combed the *Ulua* from stem and stern. They inspected every hold. They opened doors and peered into closets. They banged the butts of their rifles against boxes and tanks. When they were convinced that there was absolutely no one aboard, they left.

But there was still life aboard the *Ulua.* When darkness fell, the round cover of one of the tanks in the hold lifted slowly. Uzi thrust his head above the rim. He looked and listened a long moment, in case guards had been posted on deck. He heard only the sound of the water lapping the side of the ship. He climbed out of the tank and tapped gently on two other tanks. Out of one came Avram, head tightly bandaged. Out of the other crawled Nissan. All three crept out on deck.

Silently they lowered themselves into the water and began swimming toward shore, making a wide detour to avoid the paratroopers. They swam for about an hour, then came ashore, exhausted, in Bat Galim. The entire Haifa area was under curfew. British patrols were cruising everywhere. But the three men were familiar with the area and knew what they were looking for. They knocked on a door. They were among friends.

The next morning they reported the full story of the *Ulua* to Haganah headquarters.

Camp 66

IN THE hold of the *Empire Rival* the refugees slept the sleep of exhaustion. The next morning they rose, still suffering from fatigue and from a variety of pains and aches. We reached Famagusta at noon, and the ship dropped anchor. Shortly afterwards the doors were unlocked and armed Scottish soldiers formed two ranks. The officers asked us to leave the ship.

These soldiers were obviously less tense and aggressive than those in Haifa. Their attitude toward us was also different, more humane. We could even detect a trace of compassion in their eyes. In Palestine the British felt as though they were under siege. Here, on "their" tranquil island, they could display the victor's generosity to the vanquished and the forgiving attitude of the landowner toward homeless refugees.

We clambered aboard army trucks and, under armed guard, left the picturesque port city. A throng of Greeks and Turks lined the streets, gazing at us with mingled pity and curiosity. Here and there someone waved a handkerchief. A few miles out of town the trucks halted in front of an iron gate topped with barbed wire and bearing a large sign, in English: *Camp* 66. Gray barracks, high two-ply barbed-wire fence, sentry towers.

Again we were lined up. We were led past a row of field tents outside the gate. In the central tent were men from the British Field Security Services and the Criminal Investigation Department of the Palestine Police. They counted us, registered us, scrutinized each one, compared our faces with photographs and lists they had, interrogated us. The refugees had been trained for this ordeal while still aboard ship.

"What is your name?"

"I am a Jew from Eretz-Israel."

"What languages do you speak?"

"Hebrew."

The answers were uniform, like the questions.

We had with us a young man named Sasha, a battle-scarred soldier who had served with the Armored Corps of the Soviet Red Army. Following the war, he was swept up in Mossad operations and reached Italy. An excellent mechanic, Sasha was acquired by our men in Italy and worked for about two years with our drivers in that country. He was soon completely at ease with our men. He learned a bit of Hebrew and incidentally enriched his score of classic Russian curses with a choice selection of Arabic epithets which our men, who hailed from Yavniel, Kfar Giladi and Kfar Tabor, with many Arab neighbors, taught him with great relish. When Sasha's turn came and he was asked by the British sergeant about the languages he spoke, he replied: "Arabic." The sergeant perked up his ears and motioned to his two comrades. This one might be a real catch, perhaps one of the ringleaders of the blockade-runners. The intelligence sergeant switched to Arabic: *"Shu ismak?"* To which Sasha responded with a three-ply curse in Arabic which embraced the sergeant's sister, mother and grandmother.

We filed into Camp 66. At the first tin hut stood four men who invited us to join them inside. They identified themselves: two Joint Distribution Committee men and two emissaries from Eretz-Yisrael. The British allowed representatives of the Jewish refugee agencies as well as our own welfare workers to come to Cyprus and take care of the refugees. I recognized one of the JDC men, Joseph Schwartz, an American Jew who had worked with us in Italy. I went up to him:

"Aren't you Joe Schwartz?"

He looked at me. "That's right, I'm Joe Schwartz. Who are you?"

"Don't you recognize me, Joe?" I asked. "Take a good look."

He studied my face. "No . . . I don't know you . . . just a minute, you do remind me of someone . . . but it can't be . . ."

"Joe," I said, "my name is Arthur. We worked together in Italy."

Now he recognized me, through the bewhiskered mask of grime which covered my features. He embraced me and couldn't hold back his tears.

I turned to the emissaries from Eretz-Yisrael. I knew that one of them would identify himself as a representative of the Jewish community's national institutions, and would lead me to the Haganah agents inside the camp. While the hundreds of refugees were still filing into the camp, Yoash approached me and introduced himself as the camp commader for the Haganah. The internal administration of Camp 66—one of many—was entirely in the hands of the Haganah, which infiltrated the commanders into the camps in the guise of social workers and educators sent from Eretz-Yisrael, or planted them aboard blockade-runners with whose passengers they remained if captured. I gave Yoash a report about the *Ulua* people, our own boys, the Americans and the Spanish sailors. I estimated the number who came on the *Empire Rival* as one-third of the *Ulua*'s passengers and speculated that the others would be brought in other deportation ships.

Camp 66 was joined by an iron bridge to Camp 64, which already contained several thousand refugees from previous ships, and the veterans of Camp 64 soon came over and helped us get settled. The camp buildings were arched metal huts which resembled the "Nissen" huts used so extensively in British camps during World War II. Each hut housed several dozen refugees. There were huts for toilets, dining rooms and a kitchen. Family units were given huts divided into small cells by wooden partitions. As commander of the ship, I was assigned such a cell. I accepted it without any qualms. I was waiting for Tanya.

The refugees, who after six or seven years in concentration camps were accustomed to far worse conditions, became used to their new situation with whirlwind speed, especially since the presence of the Haganah command gave them a feeling of being at home. It took but one day to organize the service facilities and the kitchen. The people scrubbed themselves clean, laundered their clothing and regained their human appearance.

In the course of the first day, I transferred command authority over the refugees to Yoash. Together we planned the swift liberation, from the camp, of the Haganah men, the American seamen and the Spanish crewmen. The Haganah had several methods for liberating its men. We could use escape tunnels and our underground contacts in Cyprus itself, or we could place them at the head of the "release list." From time to time the British released a few hundred inmates of the Cyprus camps and permitted them to enter Palestine. The list was drawn up on the principle of "first in, first out." Since we controlled the internal administration, we advanced the ship commanders and crews to the top of the list by the use of forged documents. We thus got them back to Eretz-Yisrael and back into action again quickly.

Headquarters now asked that I return to Eretz-Yisrael immediately. According to our men, they were making the necessary preparations to release me within a week. I therefore had only a few days left in camp. I waited impatiently for the arrival of the others, including Tanya.

Another day passed. Toward evening a long convoy of trucks reached the camp. We knew that these were bringing the rest of the *Ulua* people. We watched them dismount and form a long line to the British control tent outside the camp and go through the gates. The J.D.C. people waited for them at the reception hut, and I stood near the hut together with several others of our men. We shook hands with some, embraced others. Seeing us gave their spirits a lift. Hundreds had already gone by. I was becoming more and more impatient by the minute.

"Where's Tanya? Has anything happened to her?"

One of the veteran "Swedes" came by and I put my questions to her. A mischievous gleam came into her tired eyes:

"Hey, Arthur, your Tanya is here. I saw her standing among the last in line. You'll be seeing her soon."

Tanya was standing near the hut in her ski pants and blue jacket, with her short, loose hair and her slanting eyes half-closed in the strong electric light. She saw me and a wonderful smile came to her face. My heart beat like a hammer. The blood coursed hot within me. Tanya was in my arms. I embraced her and dragged her away from the circle of light. There, in the darkness, away from everybody, I pressed my lips to hers, my face to her face, my body to hers. We clung to each other, and time had no meaning, and the ground was solid beneath our feet. I said:

"My dear Tanya, you're trembling all over. You're tired and tense. I won't interfere with your rest tonight." I led her to her hut and her friends. "Good night, beloved, a peaceful night."

The next day was crowded with activity. I went through the camp with Yoash and introduced him to the leaders of the *hachshara* groups, the "Swedes" and the "Italians." I recommended the Danish pioneer groups and the others who had proven themselves for acceptance in the combat units organized by the Haganah in the camps themselves.

I then went to Ruhama, the leader of the religious girls. Before the battle, I had handed her the gold sovereigns and the hundreds of dollars I had. She divided them among her girls and told them how and where to conceal the money on their person. She now collected our treasure and returned it to me. I handed it over to Yoash.

Toward evening I went to Tanya's hut. A tranquil, relaxing day, hot running water and the natural feminine feeling for neatness and grooming had worked wonders. Tanya appeared refreshed, her hair was in a pony tail, and she was dressed in a shirt and khaki slacks, the standard clothing distributed to the refugees from the central storehouse. The evening belonged to Tanya and me. Earlier I had spotted a small hillock near the barbed wire fence, surrounded with sparse weeds. This was virtually the only green spot in the entire gray and barren detention camp. We sat close to each other beneath the towering, threatening barbed-wire fence. The searchlights atop the four sentry towers were already lit. Bored sentries sat by their machine-guns, watching the beams traveling back and forth along the fences. In the huts the lights went out one by one. I could see Tanya's face in the glare of the searchlights.

"My dear one," I said, "tomorrow, we shall again be separated. I shall escape from the camp and go back to my work. When I get to Eretz-Yisrael, I shall go to my superiors and tell them about you. I'll tell them we're engaged. Do you agree?"

"We're engaged, Arthur," whispered Tanya, "but what has this to do with your superiors?"

"My dear Tanya, we are going according to precedent. Some of my comrades in Operation Escape also fell in love with passengers in the embarkation camps or aboard the blockade-runners. Whenever the intentions were honorable, they tried to unite them and to bring the bride-to-be to Eretz-Yisrael."

"I understand," said Tanya. "You want me to get out of here sooner."

"Yes," I said, "with the permission of my superiors. Until then, I shall keep writing to you. Every day. I'll wait for you."

"Yes, Arthur. I'll be your wife."

The next day, before I left the camp, I approached Yoash and his friends:

"You know that I have fallen head over heels in love with one of the refugees from Sweden. In Eretz-Yisrael I'm going to ask that she be brought there quickly. We want to be married."

The fellows grinned from ear to ear: "Sure, sure, Arthur, we know all about it. We've seen Tanya, a nice girl. We'll send her to you by registered mail."

"O.K., O.K.," I said. "You're nice people, too. Keep an eye on her, but gentlemen, don't overdo it."

What about the *Ulua*?

The year was 1948, and the final days of the War of Independence. We had just received uniforms, insignia, emblems. We had fought the war mostly in gray and khaki, and here we were: citizens of the sovereign state of Israel. Suddenly we were captains, majors, lieutenant-colonels—terms and ranks and insignia we hadn't as yet digested fully.

From the window of my home atop Mount Carmel I could lift my eyes and see the shore and the bay in all their glory. The freighters were back in Haifa port, still only a few, but they enjoyed the protection of our Israeli Navy's ships, former blockade-runners hastily re-equipped, armed with obsolete cannon. My eyes rested lovingly on the *Ulua*, still perched tall and proud on the reef in Bat Galim. I seemed to notice some movement near the *Ulua*—a motor boat nearby her and men on her deck. I reached for my field glasses. No doubt about it, people were climbing aboard.

I immediately got in touch with the naval base command.

"What's going on?" I asked. "What are those people doing aboard the *Ulua*?"

Yes, the commander knows all about it, I was told. He has just received an order from the port administration: the *Ulua* had been sold for scrap. They would be coming to dismantle her.

A lump came into my throat. I thanked the commander and hung up. My first thought was to phone the Ministry of Defense or even the General Staff and ask them not to touch the *Ulua*. Then I said to myself:

What will you tell them, Lova? Just because you are now a lieutenant-colonel and were once the commander of this ship—does that give you the right to interfere with what will or will not be done with the *Ulua*?"

I already knew that part of the blockade-runners fleet was being sold to scrap dealers. We were too young, too engrossed in the war to think of these ships as bits of history. The Ministry of Defense needed every penny in foreign currency to acquire arms and equipment, and the metal in the blockade-runners was a source of foreign currency.

I did not make any calls.

The next day Tanya and I drove to the Bat Galim beach. We had been married almost a year. Tanya was in an advanced stage of pregnancy. We stood on the beach, very close to the *Ulua*. We gazed at her together for the last time.

I kept myself very busy the next few days, returning to Haifa only after nightfall. I suppose I could not bear to see them take the *Ulua* apart. The dismantlers did their job thoroughly and expeditiously. When I forced myself one day to look out the window, the *Ulua* was gone.

They that go down to the sea in ships,
that deal in great waters;
They see the works of the Lord, and
his wonders in the deep.
For he commandeth, and raiseth the stormy
wind, which lifteth up the waves thereof.
They mount up to the heaven, they go down again
to the depths, their soul is melted because of trouble.
They reel to and fro, and stagger like a
drunken man, and are at their wit's end.
Then they cry unto the Lord in their trouble,
and he bringeth them out of their distress.
He maketh the storm a calm, so that the waves
thereof are still.
Then they are glad because they be quiet; thus he
bringeth them unto their desired haven.

Psalms 107:23–30

THE ROUTE OF THE ULUA
ROUTE
NORTH SEA
ENGLAND
GERMANY
le havre
Bay of
Biscay
FRANCE
SWITZERLAND
PORTUGAL
SPAIN
CORSICA
SARDINIA
ITALY
MEDITER
Gibraltar
Algiers
Philippeville
SICILY
Sousse
MOROCCO
ALGERIA
TUNISIA
LIBYA

N
borg
U S S R
OLAND
SLOVAKIA
HUNGARY
ROMANIA
BLACK SEA
UGOSLAVIA
BULGARIA
ALBANIA
Metaponto
Gallipoli
GREECE
TURKEY
SYRIA
CYPRUS
LEBANON
NEAN SEA
Haifa
PALESTINE
TRANS JORDAN
EGYPT

Glossary

aliyah—'going up'; immigration to the Land of Israel.

Eretz-Yisrael—'the Land of Israel', geographically bounded in accordance with the Bible; the traditional Jewish term for the Promised Land.

Gideonites—the name given to *Palmach* wireless operators.

hachsharah—training (primarily agricultural) for settlement in Eretz-Israel.

Haganah—underground arm of the Jewish community in Palestine organized during the British Mandatory regime for defense against attack.

Hechalutz—'the Pioneer' or vanguard, a Zionist youth organization.

kadimah—forward.

kibbutz
kvutzah } collective agricultural settlement.

mossad—institution, establishment

oleh, olim—immigrant(s) to Eretz-Yisrael

Palmach—the "shock troops" of the Haganah, disbanded when the Israel Defense Forces came into being.

Palyam—naval arm of the *Palmach*.

sabra—one born in Eretz-Yisrael (as native as the 'prickly pear').

Shalom aleichem—'peace be upon you', traditional Jewish greeting.

shu ismak?—'what is your name'? (Arabic).

Where They Are Now

Menahem ("Churchill"), an "Ada" seaman: Col. Menahem Cohen, who served in the Naval Corps of the Israel Defense Forces.

Fabi, an "Ada" seaman: Fabi Gaber, of the Prime Minister's Office.

Bezalel, an "Ada" seaman: Bezalel Drori, "Hamat" Enterprises Management.

Haim, "Ada" wireless operator: Haim Goldis, fell in the battle to break through the road to Jerusalem in the War of Independence.

Uri, "Ada" wireless operator: Lt. Col. Uri Goren, Israel Defense Forces.

Uzi, an "Ulua" seaman: Senior Commander Yisrael Auerbach, director of the Shipping Division, Ministry of Transport.

Gad, an "Ulua" seaman: Commander Gad Hilev, Chief Inspector, ZIM Israel Navigation Company Ltd.

Miri, an "Ulua" seaman: Zvi Katzenelson, Kibbutz Kfar Menahem.

Nissan, an "Ulua" seaman: Prof. Nissan Livyatan, Lecturer in Economics at the Hebrew University, Jerusalem.

Ephraim, an "Ulua" seaman: Chief Machinery Officer Ephraim Zucker, ZIM.

Avram, an "Ulua" seaman: Abraham Shavit, Moshav Kfar Vitkin.

Yeheskel, an "Ulua" seaman: Yeheskel Maoz, Ministry of Agriculture, Kiryat-Gat.

Mussik, "Ulua" wireless operator: Col. Moshe Gidron, commander of the Communications Corps, Israel Defense Forces.